Ultimate Organizational Leadership:

225 Tips from Socrates, Plato, Aristotle, and Alexander the Great

JUSTIN N. TYME

Introduction

In today's business environment, it is not ok to be just good or just great. Organizations need to hit their peak through ultimate leadership standards. More organizations are realizing that people are more important than great systems. There have been several instances of bad strategies, bad poise, and poor leadership from top to the organization pyramid to the bottom of the base. Organizational leadership is built around vision, business systems, people, and execution. Organizational leadership excels despite being buried in a bureaucratic system. The legacy of great leadership was demonstrated in ancient Greek times through generational leadership. This book demonstrates the philosophical ideals among four generations of great men who was comfortable enough with themselves that they felt empowered to develop another without ego or insecurity. Socrates taught Plato, Plato taught Aristotle, and Aristotle taught Alexander the Great.

This book should provide the following benefits:

- 219 philosophical quotes and interpretations related to business and organizational leadership from the 3 greatest philosophers of all time
- 6 bonus quotes and interpretations related to business and organizational leadership from one of the greatest military tacticians in history
- The role that communication plays into achieving the organization's objective

- When to speak up and provide feedback to the organization and HOW to do it
- How veteran team members provide solid wisdom to the next generation
- Methods for subordinates to interact with upper management
- The benefits of recruiting talent to continually advance the organization
- Explains why leaders don't need to know everything but need to perform one function really well
- True leadership withstands time and is transferred through generational leadership and not one time occurrences

Let's begin on this journey.

CONTENTS

Ultimate Organizational Leadership:

73 Tips from Socrates

Who is Socrates?

(Born 469/470 B.C. and died 399 B.C.)

Socrates is one of the most influential Western philosophers of all time. Socrates was originally very well known in Athens for his military skills in the beginning of the Peloponnesian War. He was very interested in philosophy as a young man and was taught by three female teachers (Pythia, the oracle at Delphi, Asphasia of Miletus and Diotima of Mantinea) as well as the works of Heraclitus and Parmenides. Socrates admitted that he didn't have specialized knowledge which indicated that he chose not to have a doctrine. Socrates was well respected by the young people as he challenged the elders who tried to impress the crowds with unsound arguments.

"Why are you asking all those questions?" "Can't we just keep assuming?" You can assume if you want to stay in the dark instead of walking into the light of knowledge. The Socratic Method was built on asking questions and challenging the rational of thoughts and theories to get thought provoking answers. The originator was very popular at social gathering for humbling contemporary teachers who were expert debaters. He didn't back down from challenging conventional thoughts which created political enemies for himself. In the end, those political enemies put Socrates in jail and put him to death by poison. Before he died, he held firm to his convictions and stay bold in tough circumstances although he had an opportunity to escape and venture into exile. Socrates spoke of living a good life with integrity. Put your best efforts forward and be an example to the youth with sound leadership.

Tip #1

"The only true wisdom is in knowing you know nothing."

Just because you are the leader, it doesn't mean that you have to be infallible and brilliant in every component of the business on your team. It's OK to be a leader and have gaps in your knowledge base. You just need to acknowledge those gaps and source the strengths to fill those gaps from within your team (or recruit externally). Only a fool (or resource limited person) will try to run and dictate the entire show by themselves when a team is available to help. False sense of wisdom limits the growth of your crew and turns you into a bitter leader.

Tip # 2

"The unexamined life is not worth living."

Leadership isn't about mastering all skills and being a one person show. It's about motivating individual with specialized skill sets to maximize their value to the organization. As a matter of fact, you want team members that have strengths where your weaknesses are. The goal is to create a well rounded, talent group not a kingdom filled with minions.

Tip #3

"Wonder is the beginning of wisdom."

The first principle of any organization, business, group, etc. is that it success lies in marketing. All businesses are marketing companies. They may sell similar products and services but the difference lies in the brand marketing and value added benefits. It is the wonder of this concept that limits organizational leadership success with failure to communicate this concept to the masses.

Tip #4

"I cannot teach anybody anything. I can only make them think"

Employees and society in general really prefer not to think independently anymore. It carries too much risk. They want a guide for decision making to remove the risk of independent thinking and decision making. The whole ISO (International Organization of Standards) concept was built to remove thinking and replace it with standardized instructions. It's a dummy down strategy but the selling point lies in the legality of the program. ISO provides legal protection for organizations to their suppliers, customers, employees and the public. In this example, leaders have the most impact by imploring the practice of thinking within the employees to brainstorm numerous worse case scenarios plus solutions to resolve those situations.

Tip #5

"To find yourself, think for yourself."

One of the differences between a leader and a follower lies in thinking. Followers choose not to think. Why is that? Sometimes, it lies in the experience with insecure managers. Insecure managers fear the brilliance of their staff's thoughts. The ideas are potentially so much better and on a higher plane that an insecure manager chooses to steal them rather than empower them. A leader encourages and gives credit to independent thought. A wealth of great ideas that are well developed and executed moves the organization forward so much faster if you don't mind who gets the credit.

Tip #6

"Be slow to fall into friendship, but when you are in, continue firm and constant."

Be slow to trust and reveal personal circumstances about yourself. It exposes you to risk and backstabbing down the line especially if you're interacting with shallow and insecure teammates. We all need confidantes and a support network. Make sure that they have earned your trust with real experience and tenure. Start with small and non-threatening information. How do they handle it? If they are worthy and prove themselves, then you can allow them into your inner circle. Although communication is crucial to build trust, we're talking organization business and not personal.

Tip #7

"Regard your good name as the richest jewel you can possibly be possessed of -- for credit is like fire; when once you have kindled it you may easily preserve it, but if you once extinguish it, you will find it an arduous task to rekindle it again. The way to a good reputation is to endeavor to be what you desire to appear."

Your name and your word are the most important things to protect in your brand as a leader. If you give your word to perform a task, don't use excuses…do whatever you need to do to accomplish it. Don't use the word, "try". "Try" is an excuse to not do it. Leaders are respected for keeping their word and getting the job done. Don't ask me to do more than you as a leader are willing to do.

Tip #8

"The only good is knowledge and the only evil is ignorance."

Leaders should always strive to learn more about their organization's business each week. Think about problems that faces your organizations. What are possible resolutions? When in doubt, Google that. It's surprising to find that answers surround us in our everyday lives if we can uncover the hidden links and make them practical to our scenarios.

Tip #9

"Be kind, for everyone you meet is fighting a hard battle."

Life brings challenges in many different forms in business, personal health, relationships, finances, spiritual beliefs, etc. Challenges in one area can affect us in another one. Instead of generalizing employees as lazy and trifling upon a five minute, first impression, try to dig deeper into gaining understanding why a decision or action create its current state. You may find a valid reason versus a biased opinion. Arrogance and ignorance values opinions over facts.

Tip #10

"Know thyself."

You develop a life script built upon successes, failures, and learning lessons in those experiences. Leadership involves internalizing those experiences and continuing to build upon the successes with additional knowledge, mentoring, and practice. The masses will be content with a mixed bag of results and blame the failure on anybody but themselves. It's easier to live with yourself if you don't accept the failure and are too lazy to improve yourself.

Tip #11

"If you don't get what you want, you suffer; if you get what you don't

want, you suffer; even when you get exactly what you want, you still suffer because you can't hold on to it forever. Your mind is your predicament. It wants to be free of change. Free of pain, free of the obligations of life and death. But change is law and no amount of pretending will alter that reality."

You'll never be wholly satisfied in your career. No matter what level you sit within the organization; you'll have periods of frustration with decisions that are different from your own. Organizations are bureaucratic and influence is the currency that barters the deals. As a leader, you need to persevere and be patient. Look to your opportunities to carry influence and take measured steps to communicate effectively without any animosity. Above all else, leaders are team players.

Tip #12

"Education is the kindling of a flame, not the filling of a vessel."

This tip does not refer to a formal collegiate education. It refers to a desire to seek knowledge and gain understanding from any and all sources available. You can learn from networking with industry veterans, customers, suppliers, online resources, peers, newer employees and even family members. You will never be too old to learn new information.

Tip #13

"Our youth now love luxury. They have bad manners, contempt for authority; they show disrespect for their elders and love chatter in place of exercise; they no longer rise when elders enter the room; they contradict their parents, chatter before company; gobble up their

food and tyrannize their teachers."

The next generation of workers always appears to be more disrespectful than the past ones. This is a timeless quote. Each generation grew up differently based on technological advances and observations of the past generation's work lives. If you grew up where your parents worked 80 hour per week, got laid off within 7 years of retirement, spent very little time with you as a child at home plus found out that they picked up a cancer requiring them to spend all of their golden nest egg without enjoying it, you do grow up with a different mindset. In their eyes, the previous generation's methods didn't work. Let's try something different. In any case, each generation is responsible to learn the motivation of their students and teach them to seek excellence on the next level.

Tip #14

"Death may be the greatest of all human blessings."

In this example, death refers to losing a job. In certain instances, employees will stay with an organization too long. Sometimes, there is truly a conflict with a leader's view differing from the organization's direction. It requires a change in scenery. You need to find an organization that is aligned with views (at least 80% of it). You'll be much happier in the long run.

Tip #15

"Every action has its pleasures and its price."

Decision making lies in the pros and cons of the choices. Success is defined by the pros outweighing the cons with a bigger benefit to the involved party. As a leader, you should realize that everyone will not applaud your decision especially if negatively impacts their personal situation. There is a selfish side to us all and we do look to see if we're impacted on a selfish level. For the more vain people, they feel a little more empowered to voice their displeasure. In essence, you need to hold steadfast to your decision if the pros outweighed the cons; you need to change your decision if the cons outweigh the pros.

Tip #16

"The misuse of language induces evil in the soul"

As leaders communicate a message, it can build or destroy an organization. The difference lies in the clarity, intent, and delivery of that message. An honest, concise and eloquent speech that gets to the point is well received versus a carefully crafted and manipulative one. No matter what you think; selecting to manipulate and withhold certain information is still manipulating your crew to fit your agenda.

Tip #17

"He who is not contented with what he has, would not be content with what he would like to have."

There are a lot of folks who believe that they can perform at a much higher level than their boss. Some folks really could do better but unfortunately, most can't. They're not equipped to take accountability for their decisions. They're not willing to make sacrifices necessary to move to the next level. They are a Monday morning quarterback giving criticism all day long but sit on the couch watching the game every Sunday as a spectator. It's useless jabber. If you can outperform your boss, volunteer to perform some of their key responsible activities. Learn the job first and get an insider's look. When the opportunities become available, be ready to act.

Tip #18

"I am not an Athenian nor a Greek, but a citizen of the world."

In a multinational organization (or umbrella organization with numerous brands), you are not identified solely by your direct affiliation. You are not competing with the organization for talent and sources. You are competing against external organizations around the world. We get lost in perceived enemies in our backyard rather than keep perspective and understand the real objective to move the organization forward.

Tip #19

"Do not do to others what angers you if done to you by others."

There are a lot of bad leaders who passed the same bad habits onto a new generation of leaders. Leadership is about growth and betterment. If you remember how you responded to certain characteristics of your managers, don't repeat the same bad traits. Seek to improve rather than stay at the same plateau.

Tip #20

"Prefer knowledge to wealth, for the one is transitory, the other perpetual"

What is your career goal? If it is to be CEO or President of an organization, the goal is to understand the qualities, required breadth of experiences, and network necessary to get an opportunity. It may require you to make a critical choice at a crossroad of your career. You may have to decide whether to climb in your current specialty at a higher level of pay but limited ceiling or take a chance with a responsibility in a different facet of the business in another location without a significant change in pay. In the second option, you may set the stage for a massive career shift to move towards your goals versus bumping your head on the ceiling of your specialty. Take chances and opportunities early on in your career before marriage and kids slow you down.

Tip #21

"Let him who would move the world first move himself."

Before you set the world on fire with your dynamic leadership skills, the first step is to lead yourself. Self improvement and discipline to make yourself a better person is crucial in your development to lead others. Try a 90 day goal to improve yourself in one area of life whether it's weight loss, community service, writing journal entries, getting up an hour earlier, etc. Do you have the discipline to stick it out? Can you make your world better before you impact others?

Tip #22

"Contentment is natural wealth, luxury is artificial poverty."

You can be a great leader and desire not to be the highest ranking officer in the organization. You shouldn't feel guilty. You are no less of a leader and not fearful of failure. Sometimes, we identify where we have the largest impact on the organization and it's not at the top. At times, we create a legacy of leaders that move up the organization and make larger impacts that we would have. If they were taught correctly and were well grounded, they never forget who guided them early in their careers.

Tip #23

"We cannot live better than in seeking to become better."

Each day, we must become better and encourage our teams to strive to become better each and every day as well. The day that we stall being progressive minded, we fall behind our peers who did not stop and delay their movements. Life is to be lived to the fullest extent with never ending vibrancy and excitement to begin the new day with fresh eyes for a brighter future.

Tip #24

"When the debate is lost, slander becomes the tool of the loser."

If you are involved in duel of influence and lose the battle, don't throw a tantrum and come off as a sore loser. Try to reason why you didn't win the debate. Did you have valid points? Was there sufficient justification in your argument? Did the opposing party bend the ear of a higher level influential party? Do not take one loss as a momentum ball rolling down the hill on top of you. You get up, dust yourself off, and get ready for the next decision.

Tip #25

"Envy is the ulcer of the soul."

We spend so much time watching and being jealous of other people advancing in their careers; we don't focus on our own careers, businesses, or jobs. No one sees the sacrifice that success requires of a person. No one sees the long term impact of a person that cheats the process and advance in the short term. As a person of integrity, you need to focus on yourself and develop your skill sets. You will benefit at the right time and not your time. Pray and meditate for guidance when you're in doubt that this practice works for believers.

Tip #26

"Thou should eat to live; not live to eat."

We love to do the wrong things in excess and then try to correct the path by reversing the process with deprivation. It is much easier to start the process with the correct tools, solid plan, and steady determination. You can recover from bad habits but change needs to be decisive and met with an unyielding spirit to win.

Tip #27

"The secret of happiness, you see, is not found in seeking more, but in developing the capacity to enjoy less."

We want the world on our terms but then what would we live for? Humans need to be challenged. We cause and resolve problems. We need to grow as individuals. It's like exercise. When you don't work out, your muscles get soft and flabby. You become more susceptible to illness and weakness. Instead of thriving, you fall short because you have no resistance to fight back.

Tip #28

"If you want to be a good saddler, saddle the worst horse; for if you can tame one, you can tame all."

Don't tackle the easiest problems or chase the easiest opportunities all of the time. You can't grow as a leader if you're never challenged. Good athletes can't be great if they play with mediocre talent. Good athletes become great playing with great talent and succeeding in tough situations. Great players on bad teams don't make All Star teams; it's the really good players on winning teams who make it. Think enough of yourself to deserve a spot on a talented team. You can't reach your potential if you're never tested. Reach for the moon and be among the stars.

Tip #29

"Beware of the barrenness of a busy life."

Sometimes, leaders get so caught up in the moment with busy activities that they forget to mentor and communicate with the team. When a leader appears isolated and too busy, the crew becomes disconnected and disjointed. The crew loses some work effectiveness due to wondering what's going on with the leader. A leader can be busy but not inaccessible to their crew. When that happens, the crew acts as a mirror and reflects the same behavior. As a leader, you become disconnected and disjointed lacking crucial information to make solid decisions.

Tip #30

"Employ your time in improving yourself by other men's writings so that you shall come easily by what others have labored hard for."

Reading is fundamental to receive knowledge from other's experiences. It's one thing to learn the hard way by trial and error; it's a smarter move to learn the easier way by someone else's mistakes. It saves you so much more time. If you don't have personal mentors or experienced veterans to bounce thoughts off of, then read books in your field of interest from respected authors and also be open to newer authors with different viewpoints. Sometimes, new authors have a transformational and revolutionary process that can be thought provoking for your career.

Tip #31

"From the deepest desires often comes the deadliest hate."

A person's real intention can't be denied over time. A person can only fake for so long before their real self comes to the surface. If you have a large and overbearing ego, then it will show when you have power and influence. Everyone can't handle power with humility, servitude and zeal. If you can handle it with dignity, diligence and passion, you have a good start to perform well.

Tip #32

"Enjoy yourself -- it's later than you think."

Sometimes we never stop and enjoy the moment. Most career professionals spend so much time fighting and striving for the next promotion or opportunity; they never stop and enjoy the current position. In the last years of a career, those same professionals do spend time to reflect and realize that they forgot to have fun while they had a chance. They realized that they rushed out of a wonderful position into another position that was not as satisfying. Remember to take a few minutes a day to identify the best portions of your current job and reflect on whether it is a joy and pain.

Tip #33

"Sometimes you put walls up not to keep people out, but to see who cares enough to break them down."

There are a lot of leaders that are introverts. An introvert can be perceived as shy and withdrawn but that is not the defining characteristic of that personality. Introverts are defined by their power source. Introverts draw their internal motivation and power from within themselves. Extroverts draw motivation and power from their surroundings. An introvert leader just needs a subordinate to initiate dialog, socialize on external (of work) topics and ask questions to find out how to help them succeed. The investment could create a confidante and supporter of future career moves and opportunities.

Tip #34

"Fame is the perfume of heroic deeds."

We all want credit for our successes and appreciation for putting forth effort beyond reasonable expectation but we don't necessarily receive it in a timely manner. Leaders gain a nice edge on most managers by the small things like saying "Thank you for [specify what task was completed and how it helped you and/or the organization]. It keeps your team invested in the organization's success.

Tip #35

"I pray Thee, O God, that I may be beautiful within."

As leaders, we sometimes can't see how we are being perceived by our team. If you really want to know how you're performing in your role, ask for candid feedback or set up an anonymous feedback system where your team don't have to fear repercussions. They have to trust that you will not seek payback if it's not glowing remarks. You have to be emotionally strong enough to handle the feedback without being vindictive. The truth can be painful but offer opportunities for reflection and a decision to change or stay the same.

Tip #36

"Strong minds discuss ideas, average minds discuss events, weak minds discuss people."

This tip refers to integrity and character. You'll notice that the majority of your peers are preoccupied with pettiness and negative talk. You need to find like-minded people who carry the same enthusiasm and zest to make a positive contribution. It is infectious and carries over to greater contributions and experiences.

Tip #37

"Do not trouble about those who practice philosophy, whether they are good or bad; but examine the thing itself well and carefully. And if philosophy appears a bad thing to you, turn every man from it, not only your sons; but if it appears to you such as I think it to be, take courage, pursue it, and practice it, as the saying is, 'both you and your house."

If you are not in leadership position and are unhappy with the decision making process employed, you have two real choices: (1) work towards joining the leadership ranks and make a positive change or (2) go join another organization that has a similar philosophy to your own. Don't stay with an organization and engage in negative verbal colloquiums on a daily basis. Study the decisions in silence and internally evaluate if this organization works for you or not. Be strong enough to walk away if it doesn't without compromising your character. Setting off explosions and high blazes are only attractive in action movies and not in real life.

Tip #38

"Be of good cheer about death, and know this of a truth, that no evil can happen to a good man, either in life or after death."

Don't compromise your integrity for job security. A lot of good managers sacrifice their beliefs and instincts because it doesn't fit the organization's political agenda. There is a fear of being ostracized and cast off into purgatory and dead end assignments. You'd be better off and happier with yourself if you lived according to truth and good principles. If you are escorted out of the organization, your head should be held high and move on to the next opportunity. You will definitely feel worse and suffer in silence if you ignore your moral compass.

Tip #39

"Think not those faithful who praise all thy words and actions; but those who kindly reprove thy faults."

As a leader, you cannot be surrounded by "Yes" men and women and expect to succeed. In this situation, your organization's ascent is limited by your thoughts only. An organization moves higher because the collective conscientious grows an exponential level based on thorough data collection and objective discussions. If you want to know if you're surrounded by "Yes" folks, try an example with a mildly wrong idea with a valid reason why it would in fail in your mind; what does your team do? Do they engage in a discussion or give you the green light to go ahead? If they are in the latter, you need to sit your team down for a heart to heart discussion about honesty and bring value to the organization. If some team members have nothing to offer, you need to downgrade their importance in your organization and allow someone else the opportunity to excel.

Tip #40

"We can easily forgive a child who is afraid of the dark; the real tragedy of life is when men are afraid of the light."

Some managers prefer to be ignorant of certain organization matters in fear of uncovering immoral practices. A leader wants to know if immoral practices are in place and correct those issues to increase trust throughout the organization. Movies like Matt Damon's "The Informant" is a very good example. Enron's business practices are another example that devastated thousands of its employees.

Tip #41

"If all our misfortunes were laid in one common heap whence everyone must take an equal portion, most people would be content to take their own and depart."

One fear throughout large organizations is the silo effect where specific teams would focus and put forth efforts to address concerns in their specific areas but are not too interested in the problems facing other factions of the business. The North American group may have some great ideas but didn't feel necessary to show best practices with the South American group. The Asia/Africa division may have uncovered a new technology which would have a larger impact to some of the divisions. If only, they communicated across the lines and shared knowledge freely.

Tip #42

"Esteemed friend, citizen of Athens, the greatest city in the world, so outstanding in both intelligence and power, aren't you ashamed to care so much to make all the money you can, and to advance your reputation and prestige--while for truth and wisdom and the improvement of your soul you have no care or worry?"

Social and environmental responsibility is a growing organization metric to present a well rounded view of a successful organization that can be profitable to investors and positive to the global community for long term sustainability. Look for ways to save energy and money in your organization. Look for ways to recycle material and reduce volume to landfill. Donate to charitable causes and represent the organization in a good light.

Tip #43

"The greatest blessing granted to mankind come by way of madness, which is a divine gift."

I like to think that the divine gift listed in the tip refers to tenacity. Tenacity is a guttural drive to see a problem through to its solution. The difference between success and failure in an assignment can simply come down to tenacity and follow through. It can become maddening as you dedicate a ton of hours and implore a laser like focus seeking excellence.

Tip #44

"Understanding a question is half an answer"

Leaders in unfamiliar territory are armed with their most important asset: their minds. The art of questioning is a hallmark of Socrates. Questions are used to delve down to the root cause(s) of a problem and lead to a true resolution. Most problems are based on poor decision making skills. Good questioning at the start of a project can head off potential shortfalls and traps.

Tip #45

"The hour of departure has arrived, and we go our separate ways, I to die, and you to live. Which of these two is better; only God knows."

Even if a leader identifies their perfect niche, they should not hold the same position for the bulk of their career. You have to imagine that ideas will get stale and complacency begins to step in plus old habits get formed. In the end, there should be a transition period of management movement within an organization. Most organizations prefer to have the bulk of their talent shift positions within a five year window. It keeps the staff from being complacent and encourages them to be engaged. It also gives the upper management options if turnover in key assignments become an issue.

Tip #46

"The greatest way to live with honor in this world is to be what we pretend to be."

In the start of an organization's journey, leaders need to be more visionary. In a practical sense, you must be realistic in terms of where the organization stands. Afterwards, you need to visualize and prepare for where the organization can be. You need to pretend that the organization is already acting in accord to what it can be at the pinnacle of your thoughts. If you can't envision it, neither will your team. Bring passion to the dream.

Tip #47

"The beginning of wisdom is the definition of terms."

The first step to make a difference inside the organization is to learn the rules within an organization. You've heard that rules were made to be broken but it's smarter to work magic inside of those rules. What can you do or not do? Don't jeopardize your career to be label a rebellious leader. Are you empowered to take action or are you limited in proactive behavior? Can you empower your team to take proactive actions?

Tip #48

"In all of us, even in good men, there is a lawless wild-beast nature, which peers out in sleep."

It is nice to be the calm, cool and collected team leader; ice water running through your veins despite hell surrounding you. It's nice but it can be perceived that you don't understand the depth and importance of a situation because you're focused on being cool. Your crew has to know that their fearless leader has a range of emotions to keep them in check. Show urgency when it is merited. When a mistake is made, don't ignore it;

call them on it. They'll respect you in the long run and will let new teammates know that they can't cut corners without being held accountable by you. It'll make your career move a lot easier.

Tip #49

"Through your rags I see your vanity."

You've heard the phrase about clothes making the man. Perception is very important inside organizations. Malcolm Gladwell, author of "Blink", "The Tipping Point", and "Outliers", spoke about the importance of images in business and life. The stereotypical leader is a male that is six feet tall or more with a slim build and an attractive look. If you have these characteristics, God bless you. Most folks don't but there are thousands of stories demonstrating great leaders that don't fit inside that package. As adult, we're not growing any taller in this lifetime. We can take measures to control our weight and get in better shape. We can take the time to improve our clothing wear. The common practice is to dress for the next position up in the organization so that your leadership team above your level can visualize you in their echelon of the organization. Unfortunately, we are still visual creatures.

Tip #50

"Beauty is a short-lived tyranny."

Attractive people do have an easier road to financial success, favors and opportunities in organization. It shouldn't be a crime to be blessed with good looks. It is disheartening when attractiveness is used for advancement and special assignments when the work is not merited. If you are attractive, make someone really jealous and bring a beautiful mind to the table as well. Feel free to have the whole package. Good looks fade as you get older and the favors that you're used to receiving will be dispatched to younger protégés playing the same game.

Tip #51

"To be is to do"

Sometimes it's better to do something first and then to be accountable for the results. Business folks make the term "accountability" a code word for responsible if it screws up. Accountability is really about ownership and making success a reality. You don't pass the buck. As a leader, the buck stops here and you're making plans to make it better and more effective. The intent is **to be** great and **to do** great things.

Tip #52

"And therefore if the head and the body are to be well, you must begin by curing the soul; that is the first and essential thing. And the care of the soul, my dear youth, has to be effected by the use of certain charms, and these charms are fair words; and by them temperance is implanted in the soul, and where temperance comes and stays, there health is speedily imparted, not only to the head, but to the whole body."

Although leadership is exciting and demands action, reason and logical thinking must be part of the formula as well. You must be reflective in your decision making and people interaction. Your team must be engaged by reasons that make sense to them and not just by you. You need to understand motivating and demotivating factors for your team members to get their hearts and minds working in unison to epitomize the targets of success.

Tip #53

"Well, although I do not suppose that either of us know anything really beautiful & good, I am better off than he is- for he knows nothing & thinks that he knows; I neither know nor think that I know."

Nothing is worse than the arrogant leader who refuses to listen and make decisions recklessly. It is a sure bet that negative consequences will be felt by all based on this style. The unfortunate part of business is that the tendency is to never return to what actually worked; we tend to modify and modify some more the incorrect decision that led us down the wrong path in the first place. Be willing to go back to step one if your decision causes the organization to go down the wrong path. The staff may admire you for listening to their concerns and heeding their advice.

Tip #54

"The really important thing is not to live, but to live well. And to live well meant, along with more enjoyable things in life, to live according to your principles."

Organizations really thrive when intellect is captured across a diverse landscape of people. Training is an essential ingredient to make your team realize that the organization seeks to invest in them for continual growth. It's like cultivating a beautiful garden of new knowledge and past experiences. You may not be promoted as quick as you'd like but your skill set should not be trapped in a past decade making you outdated.

Tip #55

"God takes away the minds of poets, and uses them as his ministers, as he also uses diviners and holy prophets, in order that we who hear them may know them to be speaking not of themselves who utter these priceless words in a state of unconsciousness, but that God himself is the speaker, and that through them he is conversing with us."

Charisma may seem like a sales thing when it comes to leadership but it really is important that you can attract great talent and motivate to get the best out of your team without whipping them like slaves trying to run away. You get much better results from a willing and active team than the opposite. When your team is acting in a preferred mode of business, please reward them in some form and fashion and let them know why so they stay encouraged and act in the same manner each and every time.

Tip #56

"The easiest and noblest way is not to be crushing others, but to be improving yourselves."

Don't throw rocks at another leader's organization just to steal talent away. It is a petty and backstabbing move. Karma will return the favor and you may not be ready. Leaders need to focus in their own houses and improve their current teams instead. The best case is improvement built with your current personnel but that is not applicable in most scenarios. You must invest time in team members that are motivated and willing to grow. You start to divest of the team members that are looking to collect a paycheck and have no desire to progress any further in their knowledge base. In this case, they're blocking a job position from a more ambitious person seeking to create value for the organization.

Tip #57

"He is richest who is content with the least, for content is the wealth of nature."

It is a headache to have a team member who lifestyle is dependent on overtime, large bonuses and above average pay raises. When you have a talented team member who is obnoxiously focused on pay for any special assignment or promotion opportunity, it sours a leadership team on the intentions of the individual. A company does not have the responsibility to make an employee wealthy. It is the employee's responsibility to manage their personal affairs and lifestyle. It silently sends a message that the person is reckless with finances and may compromise sound decision making if money is a factor. Don't refuse to take a business opportunity just the position didn't offer the money jump that you were looking for. It can be a career limiting moment regarding future advancement opportunities.

Tip #58

"All men's souls are immortal, but the souls of the righteous are immortal and divine."

Leadership is about creating legacies for future leaders and measuring the impact of their decisions to their respective organizations. Great and horrible leaders become immortal but average ones are easily forgotten. Most times, average leaders are forgotten because they didn't rock the boat and trust themselves to make an impactful decision. They stayed the safe course and rode out to the sunset. If you've been in any organization for more than five years, think about the leaders who have come and gone. Did they make a positive, neutral or negative impact? Did they leave an impression on you and/or the organization and why? What legacy do you intend to leave as a leader? Would you be remembered?

Tip #59

"I decided that it was not wisdom that enabled [poets] to write their poetry, but a kind of instinct or inspiration, such as you find in seers and prophets who deliver all their sublime messages without knowing in the least what they mean."

Its one thing to have a vision for your organization and it's another to energize your group to extraordinary performance level. When a leader can inspire the team to see the vision and be willing to work hard to reach it; that's a sign of genuine leadership skill. Nothing is more engaging than for someone to believe that they exceeded the odds as an underdog and powered through successfully like a running back through a goal line stance.

Tip #60

"To express oneself badly is not only faulty as far as the language goes, but does some harm to the soul."

Angry moments can be explosive and dangerous to a leader's career. I'm not talking about managing a subordinate's anger. I mean the leader's angry moments. For example, a bureaucratic decision that stalls your team's momentum and it appears that the other person or group is working against you rather than with you. It's frustrating and borderline insane but the simple things must be implored. Do not respond when you are angry. Take some time to reflect and respond on a calm accord. You can respond in a strong tone but be clear on your talking points and meet face to face so there's no misunderstanding. E-mails allow folks to speak with a tougher tone than face to face dialog. Pay attention and see if you've noticed the same thing.

Tip #61

"Not life, but good life, is to be chiefly valued."

Many folks believe the grass is greener on the other side while they're wearing dark sunglasses. Sometimes, managers become envious of leaders because of a perception of a good business life on the other side. The leader's staff must be better, more cooperative and just plain lucky. Some leaders just will not receive the proper credit because a non-leader cannot admit that their leadership skills come up short. The key is not to fall into the trap and become frustrated that you don't receive proper credit as a leader when that manager is your boss. It's tough but place emphasis on living a good life. Revenge is best served with a string of victories.

Tip #62

"He who is unable to live in society, or who has no need because he is sufficient for himself, must be either a beast or a god."

The independent micromanager has a hard time trying to develop their personnel because of a low trust factor. The manager alienates the group, loses valuable time and development opportunities. When an ambitious person isn't growing and not receiving opportunities, they either lose desire to perform at a capable or move on to another organization to prevent their spirits from being zapped.

Tip #63

"The highest realms of thought are impossible to reach without first attaining an understanding of compassion."

When leaders develop a vision for themselves and the organization, the next step is to identify the hurdles and obstacles that lie before the team. Will bureaucracy and regulations prevent the team from executing the strategy within a prescribed length of time? Are the right tools and necessary talent level in place to support reaching the objectives? Is creativity and competitiveness running side by side within the organization? These are some questions to be answered before you swing for home runs; you may need to start small and bat for single step victories to get confidence growing in the organization.

Tip #64

"I did not care for the things that most people care about– making money, having a comfortable home, high military or civil rank, and all the other activities, political appointments, secret societies, party organizations, which go on in our city . . . I set myself to do you– each one of you, individually and in private– what I hold to be the greatest possible service. I tried to persuade each one of you to concern himself less with what he has than with what he is, so as to

render himself as excellent and as rational as possible."

Title doesn't make the leader; influence does. Leaders understand this principle. A true leader can get peers and upper management to act progressively on their behalf to execute needed tasks. They're not bogged down by titles and limited by chains of command. If an idea is solid and should be considered for implementation or feedback is necessary to fine tune an idea, the leader feels responsible and communicates with tact. Title seekers are typically vain people who have little substance beyond the position.

Tip #65

"One should never do wrong in return, nor mistreat any man, no matter how one has been mistreated by him."

Stuff runs downhill. I know that I modified the actual saying but you get the gist. If your manager tears you down and reams you a new one, it is not your prerogative to pass that behavior onto your team as their leader. Great leaders can absorb these difficult blows and shield the team. Remember the sayings about leaders with big shoulders. If you need to perform a little stress relief at work in between manager's rant and communicating back to the team, walk up and down stairs to get a mild workout. Try to squeeze a stress ball to death. Drink two cups of water very slowly.

Tip #66

"Now the worst part of the punishment is that he who refuses to rule is liable to be ruled by one who is worse than himself."

Some leaders don't realize the level of skill and talent within themselves. They're humble to a fault where they don't feel comfortable taking the next step in fear of failing and doing a disservice to the organization. When those opportunities occur where an inside talent chooses not to ascend, it forces the organization to look externally for candidates which is always a gamble. Gambling can pay off or lose very big. Although not stated in political sense, it prevents the inside leader from griping and being frustrated about the choices made by the external candidate turned higher level manager. You can't complain when you didn't even choose to interview. You made a choice and so did the organization.

Tip #67

"He is not only idle who does nothing, but he is idle who might be better employed."

An employee who treats their career as a job is in trouble. A job mindset leads to fighting to establish minimum functional expectations. This happens quite a bit to former "A" level talent in the organization that is transitioned down to "B" level status. Leaders have to expend more energy to get preferred performance. Employing the mind to transition back from job to career and business focus is nearly impossible. A leader must inspire and provide some immediate opportunities that shock and reengage the creative juices within that person.

Tip #68

"There is no solution; seek it lovingly."

There are times that (internal/external) limitations and regulations forces leaders to execute a strategy that is not preferred or creates more work for your crew. As a leader, you may not agree with the strategy employed but it is the organization's desired method of operation. The best advice is to force yourself to see the value in this choice, sell the values to your crew, and look for ways to make it manageable instead of a pain in the butt.

Tip #69

"The law presumably says that it is finest to keep as quiet as possible in misfortunes and not be irritated, since the good and bad in such things aren't plain, nor does taking it hard get one anywhere, not are any of the human things worthy of great seriousness.... One must accept the fall of the dice and settle one's affairs accordingly-- in whatever way argument declares would be best. One must not behave like children who have stumbled and who hold on to the hurt place and spend their time in crying out; rather one must always habituate the soul to turn as quickly as possible to curing and setting aright what has fallen and is sick, doing away with lament by medicine."

Leaders are not successful each and every time. There is not a ratio of wins to losses to define great leadership. Some failures help motivate a larger win in the big scheme of things. The important thing is to understand that successes and failures are based on decisions, actions and execution and is not a personal identification. I know that it reads in a confusing fashion. I mean that your decision can be judged, the actions can be judged and the execution can be judged but the person should not be defined by the latest judgment. The body of work and impact to the organization is more important than the last thing done.

Tip #70

"If a man comes to the door of poetry untouched by the madness of the Muses, believing that technique alone will make him a good poet, he and his sane compositions never reach perfection, but are utterly eclipsed by the performances of the inspired madman."

Management is built and dependent on systems. A well built system can absorb talent loss and force minimum standards on staff to accomplish job requisites with consistency. It's a flawed style of thinking. It's unimaginative and the organization's success is limited. Thinking and ingenuity takes a back seat to conformity and regulations. A system is greater when leadership is sprinkled all over it like good seasoning on well cooked meat.

Tip #71

"My advice to you is get married: if you find a good wife you'll be happy; if not, you'll become a philosopher."

This tip refers to being married to the job. If you find a good organization, stick with it and be happy. If not, don't become a critic within the organization. Divorce your current organization and find another organization to marry. Happiness is too valuable to sacrifice no matter the amount of pay.

Tip #72

"And the same things look bent and straight when seen in water and out of it, and also both concave and convex, due to the sight's being mislead by the colors, and every sort of confusion of this kind is plainly in our soul."

It's true when they say that there are three sides to every story: (1) stories from two parties and (2) the truth. As a leader, you have to be real cautious when settling disputes on which side you choose to protect and defend. It is very difficult to prevent yourself from casting judgment and give the perception that you choosing a side when you need to be arbitrary. The best approach is to have both sides in the same room to discuss issues and try to identify consistencies within both stories. Most times, emotions are the key to changing a truth into a story. How a person felt during the conversation will influence what was said and how it was interpreted? As a non-bias leader, both parties need to feel support from you that a resolution is possible and that you're dealing with the behaviors and not damning the person.

Tip #73

"Remember, no human condition is ever permanent. Then you will not be overjoyed in good fortune nor too scornful in misfortune."

In business, you never know the season of leaders in your organizations. What situations seem permanent is all of sudden seems temporary. What situations seem temporary is all of sudden permanent (extremely long term). It's a game of persistence. You try not to make future personal and business decisions based on other folk's decisions. If you enjoy your job but not the leader; you really want to carefully evaluate your next move. Don't make a hasty decision. It can lead to one of the biggest regrets of your career.

Ultimate Organizational Leadership:

73 Tips from Plato

Who was Plato?

(Born 428/7 B.C. and died 348/7 B.C.)

Plato is one of the greatest philosophers that ever lived. The classic Greek philosopher was in the middle of the greatest trinity of teacher-student philosophers of all time. Socrates was his teacher and Aristotle was his student. Plato laid down the foundation for Western philosophy and science. He was an educator (specializing in mathematics, science, and philosophy) and founded the Academy in Athens which was the first institution of higher learning. Plato was recognized for transcribing 36 dialogs and 13 letters presenting his theories and communicating the legacy of his teacher. As Plato was raised under an aristocratic upbringing, he was very concerned about the quality of leadership in his state's government. He feared a decline from the most optimum form of organizational leadership which begins as (1) an 'aristocracy' which are ruled by the best leaders lowering to (2) a 'timocracy' which are ruled by the most honorable leaders falling to (3) an 'obligarchy' which are ruled by a few folks like a clique descending to (4) a 'democracy' which are ruled by many folks to finally (5) a 'tyranny' ruled by one mean dude.

Tip #74

"Be kind, for everyone you meet is fighting a harder battle."

A lot of times, we are so self- involved with our own agendas that we do not care what issues are bothering our team members (subordinates, peers, and managers). In a logic driven society, the hardships of life should not influence folks at work but human emotions are real and not to be ignored. You don't have to cater and be sensitive to all concerns of your crew but more importantly, you can't ignore them and run all over your folks. The best workplace morale lies in creating a community focused on reaching a common goal.

Tip #75

"Every heart sings a song, incomplete, until another heart whispers back. Those who wish to sing always find a song."

Everyone has a plan and dreams of a better place for themselves in society.

We have thoughts on how work should be done. The question revolves around the plans and dreams of each person matching a collective vision to the betterment of the business. You don't want divisional managers venturing off on their own agendas counter to the organization's goals.

Tip #76

"Music gives a soul to the universe, wings to the mind, flight to the imagination and life to everything."

Communication is the key element. Music represents the operating agenda that organizations provide throughout all levels. Operating agendas are benchmarks and goals that are set to specifically define success in categories by their measurement targets and deadlines. A successfully executed operating agenda is like a beautiful symphony.

Tip #77

"Wise men speak because they have something to say; fools because they have to say something."

How many meetings have you attended where a person (outside of the meeting chairperson) dominated the meeting conversation with useless dialog? Never speak in a meeting just to be heard or make your presence known. The person may reveal a level of ignorance not expected by the meeting attendees and lose credibility. Worse, they'll become a water cooler topic. If you want to contribute effectively, learn the Socratic method of questioning (Why? Why? Why? Why? Why?). Try to understand the meeting outcomes related to business success.

Tip #78

"The price good men pay for indifference to public affairs is to be ruled by evil men."

If your work environment is heavily polluted by office politics and you don't play by those rules, it can be very frustrating and makes you apathetic at times. Office politics is really about trust and group also known as cliques. Organizational behavior has embedded small pockets of communities where trust in an inner circle is comfortable. Unfortunately, everyone inside of the circle is not worthy of the responsibilities and opportunity of growth. The perception is that these people are evil and ignorant but in the end, they may just be overwhelmed and insecure. The key is to focus on your quality of work and not trying to infiltrate the inner circle. Remember the weakest link typically infects a clique and takes a chunk of them out of the picture. Be social to a clique but not identified by one. Talent and drive does win out whether it's for your current organization or another one.

Tip #79

"We can easily forgive a child who is afraid of the dark; the real tragedy of life is when men are afraid of the light."

Risk management is an expected responsibility of all leaders. Fear of managing risk is the difference between being a leader and a follower. An organization can forgive a first or second tier level employee in the initial eighteen months of employment. The tolerance beyond this point is not acceptable. The key is to secure as many facts as possible and measure against the impact of the decision. Fear to make a choice will frustrate everyone and your level of respect from your teammates goes right down the toilet.

Tip #80

"Only the dead have seen the end of war."

The 'dead' refers to former 'A' level employees who fell out of favor and got dropped out of positions of significance into mediocre positions with middle of the road responsibilities. The dangers of mismanaging risk, poor decision making, and even a change in office politics can signal the end of a promising ascending career. It's humiliating and it can make these individuals pretty bitter for a few years. They have a great wealth of experience and know the ins and outs of the business game. It is good to sort knowledge from these folks but not the sour attitude that comes with it.

Tip #81

"The heaviest penalty for declining to rule is to be ruled by someone inferior to yourself."

Leadership is about influence. If you have a position of authority within your group, don't give up your authority. Many managers will let someone more aggressive take the authority away from them because of fear to make a choice, fear of being the bad guy, or just plain old insecurity. If you're scared, go buy a dog. While you're at it, you'll be watching someone inferior giving you the orders because you didn't want to.

Tip #82

"Do not train a child to learn by force or harshness; but direct them to it by what amuses their minds, so that you may be better able to discover with accuracy the peculiar bent of the genius of each."

If you replace the child reference with subordinates, you get the picture. Cruel intentions and forceful direction from a leader will return similar karma from the subordinates. Empowerment and providing sufficient tools to accomplish tasks will return greater dividends to the organization. Figure out the motivations of your crew. If you understand your crew's motivation, you can stimulate the mind and their hearts.

Tip #83

"You can discover more about a person in an hour of play than in a year of conversation."

The best way to understand your crew is to engage them in a non-work setting (i.e. team building activity or after hours social activity). Managers typically want to keep a distance so that they don't get an emotional attachment to their employees. In these settings, you don't need to share deep secrets although I have seen employees use this technique to manipulate a manager. Inside an organization, there needs to be a balance to know the motivations of your crew but not the back story to cloud your judgment when the organization needs you the most to support its objective.

Tip #84

**"Man...is a tame or civilized animal; never the less, he requires
proper instruction and a fortunate nature, and then of all animals he
becomes the most divine and most civilized; but if he be
insufficiently or ill- educated he is the most savage of earthly
creatures."**

A well led organization will have roughly 80% of the employees functioning
at a well conditioned level of performance. There will be 10% of the
organization thriving at an elite level and the other 10% functioning at a
destructive level. The ascent of the organization rises and fall based on the
constructive behavior of the top 10% versus the destructive behavior of the
bottom 10%. The best strategy is to constantly keep engaging your top
10% to get their best efforts while seeking to get rid of the bottom 10% and
recruiting better talent.

Tip #85

**"This and no other is the root from which a tyrant springs; when he
first appears he is a protector."**

When an organization is struggling and the inmates appear to be running
the asylum, a change is screaming out to the upper management team. The
executive leadership team will not sacrifice their large bonuses and the
longevity of their careers. They will seek a heavy handed change master to
raise hell and instill fear to get things back in order. The tyrant protects the
money of the big bonus crew for a while until Plan B (an uplifting manager)
is put into place.

Tip #86

"Bodily exercise, when compulsory, does no harm to the body; but knowledge which is acquired under compulsion obtains no hold on the mind."

When information is forced onto the organization without convincing communication and a reasonable explanation, the masses will fight and pray that it is a fad. In their eyes, the situation must be temporary and tolerated until it fails or becomes a routine that can be minimized.

Tip #87

"I have hardly ever known a mathematician who was capable of reasoning."

This can be referred to some of the business minded folks who have not honed their craft or continuously improved their knowledge despite their pedigree and organization ranking. Bad decisions are crippling to an organization. Corporate and Manufacturing processes are constantly battling over decision making regarding maximizing gross profits now versus reinvesting in the business now. If you harvest your current assets now without reinvesting in predictive maintenance, you could pay a steep price later. If you don't meet your obligations to the investors with predicted profit margins, a publicly traded company will find itself in a more desperate position requiring more drastic changes.

Tip #88

"Never discourage anyone...who continually makes progress, no matter how slow."

Everyone is not a quick learner. Just because someone is slower to learn, it does not mean that their learning curve and contributions will not be higher. Organizational leadership looks at the depths of the individual's ability and the conversion of that ability into actions. Those actions carry the strength of the organization. A willing soul can bring dedication and loyalty if they are nurtured and empowered. They will prove invaluable to the organization if their attitude is really good.

Tip #89

"good people do not need laws to tell them to act responsibly, while bad people will find a way around the laws"

Human resource policies are written legal agreements made to protect the organization against human biases. There are as many noble and honorable people as they are scrupulous and manipulative ones. Rules are made to fight the latter. In a litigious society, organizations need to be very careful and provide specific guidelines because this generation of workers feels entitled to unearned rights. Review your organization's policies to gain better understanding. The most important thing is to document as much as you can. Documentation wins so many cases because our memory can be clouded and details lost in the fog.

Tip #90

"Those who tell the stories rule society."

The very best salespeople are excellent story tellers. A well told story is designed to generate an emotion and connect to your target audience. As little kids, we loved it when an adult read to us. We were engaged and our imagination took us to another world. It's no different as adults. We want to hear a great story and be sold. As a professional, learn how to tell great stories. Practice story telling in small circles and one-on-one conversations until your confidence grows to larger stages.

Tip #91

"Ignorance, the root and stem of every evil."

Decision making is a critical skill in management and leadership. The present and future state of the organization is built upon sound decision making and execution. A crucial element of decision making lies in evaluating the data. Lack of or poorly secured data puts a leader at a disadvantage when needed to make a call. Instead of minimizing the risk, you praying for luck and sound gut call.

Tip #92

"I know not how I may seem to others, but to myself I am but a small child wandering upon the vast shores of knowledge, every now and then finding a small bright pebble to content myself with."

A leader is more appreciated by the team when it is perceived that the leader is knowledgeable on various aspects within the organization. No leader knows every function within their workgroup. They need to know enough of the details to keep subordinates and peers honest in their interactions. Since the devil is rooted in the details, it is a good practice to spend some time and learn elements of different job functions. Never be content with your level of understanding. Always seek to learn more and stay a student of the game.

Tip #93

"When men speak ill of thee, live so that nobody will believe them."

Rumors, gossip, and negative talk poses a risk to the morale of any organization. It is dangerous and hinders the progress of forward movement. The root cause is typically due to a lack of communication at different levels. If a person is the target of negative talk, you have two choices: (1) you can prove them right and seek revenge for exposing you or (2) you can take the higher road and focus on continuous self improvement. My advice is to determine if the rumors hold any weight. If so, work on that deficiency in present and future scenarios. If not, continue with the second choice to get stronger as a valued member within the organization.

Tip # 94

"There are three classes of men; lovers of wisdom, lovers of honor, and lovers of gain."

There are very few stellar workers that can excel in different disciplines within the organization. Sales people will typically not serve as accountants.

Accountants would typically struggles as manufacturing production manager. Quality professionals may not transition well into a Supply Chain role. Although you have engineers (and other non business degree professionals) going to graduate school to get a MBA, it doesn't guarantee a successful transition in a different discipline. The goal is to parlay it into an opportunity and discover the location of your strengths.

Tip #95

"Man is a being in search of meaning."

Whether a person has a job or a career, they want to know and understand how their contributions add to the overall business success. If the employee understands how their daily activities and decisions translate to profits and losses, they will be more conscientious of their activities. Consider posting daily information in the local area so everyone is on the same page. If an employee is kept in the dark and given direct orders to execute functions, the organization results are limited to the boss who shouts the instructions. An empowered, self directed organization moves faster and garners more success than a bureaucratic, heavily constructed one.

Tip #96

"How can you prove whether at this moment we are sleeping, and all our thoughts are a dream; or whether we are awake, and talking to one another in the waking state?"

'Numbers don't lie but liars figure' is the appropriate adage for this reference. Lean, Six Sigma, and the Theory of Constraints are business systems that promise large rewards but the results are not always quantified. Lean promises to remove wasteful actions and costs. Six Sigma promises to limit variation and prevent losses. The Theory of Constraints seeks to direct the focus of efforts on business limitations. A particular project may succeed and show value on paper but in the overall scheme, results may reveal that there was no significant impact to the overall business.

Tip #97

"I'm trying to think, don't confuse me with facts."

The future of the organization can not stay static if the facts aren't available. At that point, time becomes the enemy. Good solid facts are concrete evidence that can't be denied. Facts aren't the only components in decision making. The strategy, systems, and values of the organization must also play a role. What is the vision and how does it measure against the facts?

Tip #98

"The man who makes everything that leads to happiness depends upon himself, and not upon other men, has adopted the very best plan for living happily. This is the man of moderation, the man of manly character and of wisdom."

Passion is an invaluable tool to get the best out of you and your team but it has managed well. It can be your way all the time. The organization is a collective body with unequal levels of power and influence. The business vision, decisions, and strategies may differ from your viewpoint. It may be right or it may be wrong in your view. Although you may disagree, you cannot publicly display discontent with the organization's direction.

Leaders and influential members may disagree with decisions from time to time but they support and put forth a great effort to support the collective versus take their figurative ball and go home. You need to know that your teammates are all in at all times and not a question mark when you need them most.

Tip #99

"If women are expected to do the same work as men, we must teach them the same things."

This is still a gender bias society where women are still unfairly treated and left behind. From a perception standpoint, women cannot be considered assertive. They are considered either aggressive or passive. She can't win. Some men are hesitant to trust and give worthwhile responsibilities to women. This is a fatal flaw in organizational leadership. Women are stereotypically identified as excellent multi-taskers. This is an excellent skill to be utilized.

Tip #100

"Education is teaching our children to desire the right things."

In this scenario, let's substitute employees for children. Continuous improvement throughout the organization is the lifeblood for optimal success. A well defined operating agenda and the knowledge of how to achieve the results can help bridge the gap from nonchalant and apathetic crew to an engaged workforce.

Tip #101

"In politics we presume that everyone who knows how to get votes knows how to administer a city or a state. When we are ill... we do not ask for the handsomest physician, or the most eloquent one."

Just because a person has the position of authority, it doesn't mean that they know how to lead. There are a lot of leaders who are not trained on how to be a leader. There are a lot of managers who are not trained on how to be a good manager. A lot of the time, leadership is an on-the-job training program especially for some of the younger leaders in the organization. You need to recognize that there are deficiencies with the upper management team. They are not perfect examples of leadership. It's a fact. You can work with and influence your immediate manager by providing input as long as the manager is open to feedback. It must be delivered respectively so that their ego isn't bruised. If the manager or environment isn't conducive to feedback upward in the organization, they'll learn the hard way. Experiences will generate humility or bitterness. If you are the leader, you must allow a subordinate or peer to give you feedback to improve your own skill sets.

Tip #102

"Death is not the worst that can happen to men."

For some adults with family responsibilities, obligations, and/or perceived high self value, death is not the worse thing that can happen. It's unemployment. Unemployment is extremely difficult to understand, frustrating, and humiliating. It's hard to understand if the failure is rooted in the organization communicating the level of expected performance to the workforce or the employee desiring not to expend the necessary energy to bring the required value or attitude to the table. It could even be a result of bad leadership decisions that carried a devastating cost to the organization as a whole dragging down several casualties in the ashes of the aftermath.

Tip #103

"The soul takes nothing with her to the next world but her education and her culture. At the beginning of the journey to the next world, one's education and culture can either provide the greatest assistance, or else act as the greatest burden, to the person who has just died."

This refers to switching jobs in an organization or another company. Bad habits will reveal itself in a different environment. If the previous management team allowed employees to go unsupervised or loosely supervised, the best of one's thinking becomes the conventional route. Short cuts are taken and development is limited. Every great leader desires to mentor and generate the next great leader like a chain of stores. General Electric has set the standard for an organization's leadership development.

Tip #104

"Excellence" is not a gift, but a skill that takes practice. We do not act "rightly" because we are "excellent", in fact we achieve "excellence" by acting "rightly".”

The greatest athletes ever known combined God given talent with an overabundant drive for excellence grounded in training and practice. As Sports fans, we cheer and demand a lot from our athletes. We want to work hard during the offseason, add more to the game each year, and be a role model for our families. We expect so much work from them but we don't expect much from ourselves. We need to get off of the sidelines and get in the game. We need practice our skill sets every day. If you can't lead yourself to practice self discipline and execute your organization's strategies, then you can't lead your staff to conquer difficult goals.

Tip #105

"Character is simply habit long continued."

Persistence and resilience are underrated. Society needs satisfaction on an instant basis. Very few people desire to work hard unless they are guaranteed an opportunity to advance in a prescribed amount of time. The thinking is that you rather take advantage of the organization before they take advantage of you. In the end, neither side benefits from the person's tenure. When the leader is away, it is not time to play…it is business as usual.

Trust is often a product of your character and your actions.

Tip #106

"Necessity is the mother of invention."

If the organization has a vision but not a plan, it'll work to devise one suitable to meet the vision. If you don't have a vision, you're doomed to follow someone else's plans for you. The beautiful part about responsibility is the opportunity to be empowered and creative to achieve the organization's goals.

Tip #107

"A hero is born among a hundred, a wise man is found among a thousand, but an accomplished one might not be found even among a hundred thousand men."

This quotes lies in the recruitment strategy. Take your time to find the person who is the right fit with the potential to grow at least one level higher if not two. Sometimes, we get into such a rush to fill a position; we settle on candidates that barely meet the qualifications and worse, may never grow beyond the hired position. This is a devastating blow to a growth oriented organization. Let's go for the hero and not the zero.

Tip #108

"But Above all things truth beareth away the victory"

Fear of job security sometimes keeps us from expressing an opinion to our managers. A manager does not want to embarrass him or herself in public. They would rather get feedback on an upcoming situation prior to its unforeseen circumstance. The skill is conveying the message in a respectful way which is in a private setting where you mention an observation and provide one or two ideas to correct it in case it happens. You'll communicate a concern and position yourself and the organization to keep thriving with ego in the way.

Tip #109

"Good actions give strength to ourselves and inspire good actions in

others."

A well executed strategy gives way to success. When an organization can achieve small successes on a consistent basis, it gives you courage to chase larger goals.

Tip #110

"Courage is knowing what not to fear."

A veteran business person can look at his/her career in their rear view mirror and point to several examples where it appeared that the sky was falling and the most devastating event ever was happening to them. In the end, they got through those moments because they addressed the risks and diligently worked through it. In the moments when they failed, fear griped them and they took a backseat to the action like a leaf in the wind.

Tip #111

"You should not honor men more than truth."

In organizations, you should not expect your leadership team to be perfect. They're not perfect. They are flawed and they make mistakes. Don't blindly follow leadership into an obvious trap. Call the instructions into question or change camps as soon as you can if the leadership isn't interested in receiving feedback.

Tip #112

"The man who finds that in the course of his life he has done a lot of wrong often wakes up at night in terror, like a child with a nightmare, and his life is full of foreboding: but the man who is conscious of no wrongdoing is filled with cheerfulness and with the comfort of old age."

We always wonder if the jerks in our organizations realize that they are truly jerks. The answer is yes. The jerk's mindset is so jaded that they believe that they must act like a jerk to keep from being taken advantage of. In fact, karma gets drawn into the picture. They create the scenario where folks that interact with them believe that they have to be a jerk just to something they need. In the end, the jerk enjoys small victories but lives a miserable life.

Tip #113

"The measure of a man is what he does with power."

This quote refers to finding out the truth behind the development a person. No one is born a leader or manager. You have life experiences, mentoring and understanding up to the point where you receive an opportunity. The quality of those lessons will be reflected and revealed in the early days of leadership. You find out if you're a leader of character or leader obsessed with ego. If you have to tell someone that you're the manager, you probably fall into the second category.

Tip #114

"There are two things a person should never be angry at, what they can help, and what they cannot."

Folks in any organization like to limit their contributions and play victim whenever they don't get their way. They fall into anger and bitterness. Instead of responding to situations, they react and lose control. Perspective and Meditations are the keys. You need to understand where influence begins and end. You can't force everyone to follow your directions. You provide your input and understanding that the organization may head in a different direction. Focus on being the best teammate that you can be without obsessing over different decisions or personnel.

Tip #115

"An empty vessel makes the loudest sound, so they that have the least wit are the greatest babblers."

Ignorance is best kept quiet until the necessary knowledge can be gained. Unfortunately, some feel that leadership must have a vocal presence whether it's intelligent or not. That's not true. Ask questions in private and build up a foundation in unfamiliar territories before making public comments. Although there is the familiar saying that there are no dumb questions, that's not entirely true in business. There are no dumb questions asked in private (one-on-one). There are dumb questions asked in public view for everyone to make snap judgment and banter. Be cautious.

Tip #116

"...if a man can be properly said to love something, it must be clear that he feels affection for it as a whole, and does not love part of it to the exclusion of the rest."

This quote refers to how a leader deals with his team and the impact of favoritism. Favoritism can destroy a well functioning team. If a leader loves his team and treats them fairly, they will perform in one accord. A leader must not show favor to specific people and exclude the rest of the crew. Bitterness and betrayal will begin to overtake the comradery and failures are on the way.

Tip #117

"What a strange thing that which men call pleasure seems to be, and how astonishing the relation it has with what is thought to be its opposite, namely pain! A man cannot have both at the same time. Yet if he pursues and catches the one, he is almost always bound to catch the other also, like two creatures with one head."

Work is considered a pain. Goofing off is considered a pleasure. The majority of the average organization will engage in goofing off more than working. In an 8 hour day, the typical employee really works about 5 hours out of an 8 hour shift. In the employee activates work for just one more hour, the organization increases its output or service by 12.5%. Leaders get forced into the boss role when employees choose to be typical versus honoring the working relationship. The working relationship is a pay for service deal. You receive 8 hours of pay for 8 hours of work. This is the agreement made by the organization and the individual upon hire. Are you an honorable employee or an advantageous slacker within the organization?

Tip #118

"You know that the beginning is the most important part of any work, especially in the case of a young and tender thing; for that is the time at which the character is being formed and the desired impression is more readily taken....Shall we just carelessly allow children to hear any casual tales which may be devised by casual persons, and to receive into their minds ideas for the most part the very opposite of those which we should wish them to have when they are grown up?

We cannot....Anything received into the mind at that age is likely to become indelible and unalterable; and therefore it is most important that the tales which the young first hear should be models of virtuous thoughts...."

The first 90 days of one's career is the most important time to evaluate whether the newest contributors will be an asset or liability to the organization. It is the responsibility of each organization to put an effective plan in place to teach, provide, and challenge new employees within the first three months of service. You don't want to find out that you have a dud after investing eight months of training, meetings, and non challenging assignment. The intent is to condition new employees to the real environment and secures contributions right away. Leaders don't want new employees to obtain bad habits under their care.

Tip #119

"If men learn this, it will implant forgetfulness in their souls; they will cease to exercise memory because they rely on that which is written, calling things to remembrance no longer from within themselves, but by means of external marks. What you have discovered is a recipe not for memory, but for reminder. And it is no true wisdom that you offer your disciples, but only its semblance, for by telling them of many things without teaching them you will make them seem to know much, while for the most part they know nothing, and as men filled, not with wisdom, but with the conceit of wisdom, they will be a burden to their fellows."

Thinking is one of the hardest facets for any organization because so few choose to engage in the process. This is true in personal life. Most of us want to be told what we want, what's good for us, who we should listen to, where we should live, how we should live, etc. In business at any level from the ground level to the CEO, very few participants choose to think. Instead, they try to find historical documents to guide them or get input from technological devices to stay busy so that they have an excuse why they couldn't think at the moment.

Tip #120

"Any man may easily do harm, but not every man can do good to another."

In the industrial age, organizations were very profitable but not very responsible with regards to a negative impact to the environment. In the technological and social age, we expect organizations to be economically responsible but also social responsible with positive impact to the environment. We want organizations to be sustainable over the long term. We're finding that not all organizations are creative enough to accomplish new sustainable efforts.

Tip #121

"The beginning is the most important part of the work."

Although this is a repeat quote, there is a different interpretation for this tip. In accomplishing a new assignment, the first step is to follow one of Stephen Covey's "7 Habits for Highly Effective People". "Begin with the End in Mind." Once the final outcome has been decided and issued downward the organization chain, the leadership team must figure out effective ways to generate momentum and improve the chance for success. Most times, this involves a kick off meeting with team members and setting milestones (accomplishments by designated dates) to measure progress. In the end, planning is the most important step to accomplishing your work.

Tip #122

"It is our duty to select the best and most dependable theory that human intelligence can supply, and use it as a raft to ride the seas of life."

This could be relevant to selecting the best and most dependable folks to recruit and retain in a growing organization. In this type of organization, the human resource department is a critical facet of the recruitment process. The best organizations have premier talent that is engaged, challenged, and successful.

Tip #123

"People are like dirt. They can either nourish you and help you grow

as a person or they can stunt your growth and make you wilt and die."

The morale of your organization tells the story of effective or ineffective leadership. A demotivated crew will make work unbearable and a chore. Ideas get buried and lost forever. A motivated crew engages everyone and makes you happy to come to work. Creative ideas are exchanging and flowing like water. If you have whiners and naturally pessimistic people in your organization, you need to really evaluate if the talent and contributions really offset their filthy attitude. Sometimes, absence of a cancerous personality can become an addition because the other teammates are happier and more spirited to make up the loss.

Tip #124

"All is flux, nothing stays still"

Change is imminent and guaranteed yet we still have problems with it as a society. Nothing is the same since we were born. I'm not saying that all change is good. I'm saying that change is always coming. You want to take part and help mold the change instead of being resistant and fighting it. An employee that fights change instead of work to guide it becomes an expendable employee. No leader wants to fight all the time with a person stuck in the past. You'll be on the sidelines believing you were screwed instead of realizing that you screwed yourself but refusing to acknowledge a common law.

Tip #125

"False words are not only evil in themselves, but they infect the soul

with evil."

Communication is so important to an organization that progress will easily be stifled. Different leaders believe power is tied into being a gatekeeper of information. Leaders who keep their team in the dark over the mission of the organization will not prosper.

Tip #126

"When the tyrant has disposed of foreign enemies by conquest or treaty and there is nothing to fear from them then he is always stirring up some wary or other in order that the people may require a leader."

If you've worked in one place long enough, you've seen different styles of leadership. Most times, you'll see alternating leaders that are either stern enforcers or pleasant democratic styles. Very heavy handed leaders may be needed at certain times during the life of the organization to get through a difficult time but the effectiveness is short term. In time, that style of leadership loses all of its supporter and regress by mutiny. When this happens, the organization decides to remove that person and bring in an alternating personality to reengage the workforce.

Tip #127

"Is there a perfect world?"

In your personal life, it's not a perfect world; it's not the case in business either. You shouldn't expect it to be so. Great organizations make their mark by dealing with variations and exceeding outsider's expectations.

Tip #128

"The first and best victory is to conquer self"

Remember the first step to leadership is to lead yourself to be the very best that you can be. If you have no discipline to make yourself, you should not expect your crew to do any better. Decide on an area of life that needs improvement and make the change. Stay diligent and persistent. Make it a habit. Gain confidence in your ability to lead yourself so you can prepare to lead someone else.

Tip #129

"There's no chance of their having a conscious glimpse of the truth as long as they refuse to disturb the things they take for granted and remain incapable of explaining them. For if your starting-point is unknown, and your end-point and intermediate stages are woven together out of unknown material, there may be coherence, but knowledge is completely out of the question."

Status quo has a beginning but the question always goes back to the origin. The majority of the organization does not like to disturb the status quo because they fear where the change will take them. They believe that there was a valid reason but there is no documentation and history to explain it. In essence, no knowledge is gained or retained; it becomes a matter of insecurity when a change agent comes along with an idea.

Tip #130

"And whenever any one informs us that he has found a man who knows all the arts, and all things else that anybody knows, and every single thing with a higher degree of accuracy than any other man – whoever tells us this, I think that we can only imagine him to be a simple creature who is likely to have been deceived by some wizard or actor whom he met, and whom he thought all-knowing, because he himself was unable to analyze the nature of knowledge and ignorance and imitation."

In the first year of a new leader or subordinate, we give them the benefit of the doubt and like a shiny new object, we marvel at all of the little things that get done. As long as the new person isn't overbearing or withdrawn, we want to see them succeed and prosper in hopes that the hiring managers made the right choice. No one wants to fail or see their choices come up short. This is why the first 90 days for a new team member is the most crucial for an organization. The leadership team needs to know quickly if they uncovered an asset or a liability.

Tip #131

"We are like people looking for something they have in their hands all the time; we're looking in all directions except at the thing we want, which is probably why we haven't found it."

When new positions open up in an organization, there are two routes that an organization can partake: (1) hire talent from within the organization and (2) hire talent outside the organization in the marketplace. There are pros and cons to both strategy and the best way may be a blended effort. Unfortunately, there are organizations that fall in love with hiring talent outside of the organization beyond a healthy level (more than 30%). This activity suggests that the organizational leadership cannot develop its own leaders and needs to steal talent from other companies. In this case, the odds are good that you'll be overpaying for the choice.

Tip #132

"All I really know is the extent of my own ignorance"

A good leader knows that he doesn't need to know everything. A better leader will surround him or her with personnel that know more than themselves in certain aspects of the team's business. A leader will ascend only as high as the talent beneath can take him so you want to load up with the best talent; never mind the insecurity and false ego. The key lies in asking the right questions and being able to read if your team is truthful. You learn to ask the right questions by simply asking "why?" Why did you choose this particular decision? What are the benefits? Is this the best option and why? Pursue the "why" chain at least five times which follows the Socratic method of questioning (an obvious nod to Plato's teacher).

Tip #133

"Time is the moving image of reality"

It seems that the older we get, the faster that time flies. In reality, the speed of time never changes; our purpose changes over time. When we find a purpose for living and creating a legacy, there aren't enough hours in the day to get it done to your satisfaction. It is a battle to spend time in the wisest methods possible for the organization when everyone believes that their concern is number one. The best bet is to prioritize by (1) request made by most influential person, (2) request that are geared towards fire fighting, and (3) request that benefits the organization the most.

Tip #134

"Honesty is for the most part less profitable than dishonesty"

In the short term, it does seem that liars prosper and honest people with integrity get shafted. Notice that I stated in the short term; I do not state a particular time but liars do not prosper forever. They will be exposed at some point before retirement and the fall from grace will catch them off guard. If you need an example, read up on the Enron executives.

Tip #135

"True opinions are a fine thing and do all sorts of good so long as they stay in their place; but they will not stay long. They run away from a man's mind, so they are not worth much until you tether them by working out the reason. Once they are tied down, they become knowledge, and are stable."

Respect is a two way street between leaders and followers. Ideas, opinions, and feedback should be freely exchanged between both parties with the intent to better the organization as a whole and not for selfish purposes.

Tip #136

"[there are] two kinds of things the nature of which it would be quite wonderful to grasp by means of a systematic art...

the first consists in seeing together things that are scattered about everywhere and collecting them into one kind, so that by defining each thing we can make clear the subject of any instruction we wish to give...

[the second], in turn, is to be able to cut up each kind according to its species along its natural joints, and to try not to splinter any part, as a bad butcher might do...

...I myself am a lover of these divisions and collections, so that I may be able to think and to speak."

The expansion and divesting of assets are difficult decisions made within any organization. It is an art form with long term impact so it's not taken lightly. The short term and long term financial stability must be considered from all standpoints. You need the best of all disciplines to conduct proper risk and market analysis to confirm or deny the direction of the organization for a better future.

Tip #137

"He who approaches the temple of the Muses without inspiration, in the belief that craftsmanship alone suffices, will remain a bungler and his presumptuous poetry will be obscured by the songs of the maniacs."

Charisma and inspirational speeches are a leadership responsibility that draws emotional power from within the ranks. We have five senses plus an emotional sense that can drastically rise or fall depending on the motivation delivered with the incoming message. Toastmasters International still is a good alternative for professionals to practice speech making and delivery. Contact them at their website: www.toastmasters.org.

Tip #138

"The direction in which education starts a man will determine his future life"

The amount of work that a new employee puts into his or her career in the beginning will provide a strong indication on long term career success or failure. Beat the boss into work by about 10-15 minutes and stay as long as they do or fifteen minutes longer. If you have a manager that has no life but work, then limit yourself to no more than 60 hours in a week.

Tip #139

"Ideas are the source of all things"

An organization starts off as a vision or thought. Ideas are built around the vision developing into a mission and strategy for execution. Ideas are catalyst for a brighter future that employs more skilled folks to execute the plan. If you spent a minimum of 15 minutes a day for 14 days focused on ideas to help existing retail businesses market better products or service to its customer, you would be overwhelmed by the sheer volume of your proposals.

Tip #140

"All learning has an emotional base."

If we're fortunate and God blesses you with five senses (hearing, sight, smell, touch, and taste) & a functional mental capacity, you are truly blessed. The sixth sense is traditionally called gut instinct or intuition. I'd like to say that there is a seventh one and that is emotion. Emotion drives us to be happy or sad, inspired or depressed, responsive or reactive, etc. When an organization engages in a learning culture, the drive is to engage the mind and elevate the organization's intelligence capacity.

Tip #141

"the only thing he ought to consider, if he does anything, is whether he does right or wrong, whether it is what a good man does or a bad man"

Leadership requires tough decision making at times. It may not be the popular choice but it may be the best choice for the organization. You just got to look at the pros and cons of the choices that you'll make.

Tip #142

"That's what education should be," I said, "the art of orientation. Educators should devise the simplest and most effective methods of turning minds around. It shouldn't be the art of implanting sight in the organ, but should proceed on the understanding that the organ already has the capacity, but is improperly aligned and isn't facing the right way."

New program and employee orientations are best conveyed in a deliberate approach. First, sell the end result(s) and how it will help the masses fulfill their objectives. Second, you want to educate your folks on the benefits to the business to encourage well rounded growth and development. Don't focus on the business and neglect your crew. You'll lose them quick.

Tip #143

"The soul of him who has education is whole and perfect and escapes the worst disease, but, if a man's education be neglected, he walks lamely through life and returns good for nothing to the world below."

If you do not reinvest in your existing team, their growth as functional members in your organization has stopped cold. You must reinvest knowledge on new technology and programs to continue your organization's ascent to a more sustainable future. You can't prosper on old knowledge. When changes comes through, you create a cap that may force your clients to seek a more innovative and progressive group.

Tip #144

"Lack of activity destroys the good condition of every human being"

Lack of physical activity makes your muscles fail and become soft. Lack of mental activity makes your mind grow slower and less focused. Challenging goals are needed to stimulate creativity, competition, and confidence. Without challenges, there is no growth and greater yet, there is a fear of withering away to dust.

Tip #145

"Knowledge unqualified is knowledge simply of something learned."

I have an example. There are a lot of people who has become Six Sigma trained and qualified but have no actual experience using their training. On a resume', they listed being a Six Sigma green or black belt with little experience to back it up other than learning the terminology and getting a certificate. The idea is simple; only applied knowledge and real experiences hold value. Everything is practice and theory which has no real basis in the business world.

Tip #146

"A sensible man will remember that the eyes may be confused in two ways - by a change from light to darkness or from darkness to light; and he will recognize that the same thing happens to the soul."

As an organizational leader, you may not be the ultimate shot caller but you have enough influence to impact change and be reflective to deal with changes that aren't desirable. In the end, we all have choices to respond or react to situations. Make a choice to respond and take control of life. Be victorious.

Ultimate Organizational Leadership:

73 Tips from Aristotle

Who is Aristotle?

(Born 384 B.C. and died 322 B.C.)

The name origin of Aristotle means "the best purpose". Aristotle is considered by many people as the greatest philosopher of all time. He is third in a generation of great philosophers (Socrates-Plato-Aristotle). At the age of seven, Aristotle's father sent him to join the Academy and become a student of Plato over a twenty year period. Aristotle began as a student, graduated to researcher, and then became a teacher. He studied as many subjects as possible and provided contributions to all of them. When an opportunity to take over Plato's academy was given to Aristotle's nephew instead of him, Aristotle left to begin his own path. He established a branch of Plato's Academy and served as the lead instructor. During this period, Aristotle becomes more of his own man with his own thoughts as well. He left to become a teacher to the thirteen year old Alexander the Great. Aristotle studied and practiced every branch of science. He established his own academy in Athens called the Lyceum like his teacher but he focused more on the sciences rather than mathematics like Plato. Aristotle was forever a lifelong student that focused on learning and continuous improvement.

Tip #147

"Knowing yourself is the beginning of all wisdom."

Make a list of things that you like and don't like within your organization. If everything works out alright, the ratio of good to bad is 75-80% good. If it's a 50-50% mix plus or minus 10%, then you need to start networking and looking for another organization to make your mark. You have to know what makes you happy and ready to contribute in a positive way to the organization. Happiness can't be overvalued even if you were earning six figures or more.

Tip #148

"Some men are just as sure of the truth of their opinions as are others of what they know."

You can't be prosperous by cost cutting alone. Cost cutting can only go so far towards the floor before your business needs to be stimulated by innovation. Innovation cannot begin until you can separate specific facts and details from general assumptions and opinions. It is very important to listen to your customers and understand the market needs. In this case, you're listening for potential to create value added benefits that customers are willing to pay a slight premium.

Tip #149

"It is the mark of an educated mind to be able to entertain a thought without accepting it."

The most important thing that college teaches a student is how to think. Prior to college, students learned to memorize and regurgitate a volume of different ideas and information. Thinking is underrated. The thinking person will always have a distinct advantage in life and career over the masses who chooses to be spoon fed information. A spoon fed person can be led anywhere by anybody at anytime. They are a victim in waiting.

Tip #150

"We are what we repeatedly do. Excellence, then, is not an act, but a habit."

We attribute that God given talent alone is the saving grace to excellence. God may provide the natural ability but he expects you to work hard and maximize those talents to benefit others. Natural skills only go so far before hard work and perspiration take it to a higher platform. Athletes practice from the time that they were small children and continue in their professional careers until retirement. When you don't practice the fundamentals and creates habit, you become forced to think too much and react too quickly in critical situations where you've just lowered your odds for success. Habits allow your body to respond while your mind remains free to perform other untrained tasks.

Tip #151

"Happiness depends upon ourselves."

Happiness should not be dependent on the organization decision tree, size of staff, position in the organization, annual income, bonuses, material possessions, company perks or any other external influences. Life is accentuated by perks and extras but it shouldn't define your base happiness. A common problem in organization revolves around the paycheck. For the vast majority, the paycheck never seems to be enough. The annual raise never seems to be high enough. The overtime doesn't pay enough or the bonus seems too small relative to the CEO. A lot of workers truly do not want the responsibilities of a CEO; they just want the pay and perks. We criticize CEOs for the benefits that they receive but we don't understand what sacrifices were made and currently made now. Most CEOs don't live like rock stars but they do hustle very hard with little sleep and high levels of stress. The best advice to stop being bitter about someone else's situation unless you're willing to do whatever it takes to get there. Go to school. Read books. Get polished in business etiquette and enjoy the journey.

Tip #152

"Hope is a waking dream."

The Reverend Jesse Jackson once had a slogan called "Keep hope alive." Hope is unseen optimism for better things to come. You may not have a plan at the moment of a crisis when a business variation pops up but hope serves as a transition piece until a plan can be developed and/or a prayer can be offered up. Traditional organizations can't stand hope because it doesn't operate under concrete plans. People need hope to carry on and keep working even when they're in a rut. Why? They work with the hope of a better day and better things on the horizon. Leaders instill hope with their people. A better day always come when hope is found.

Tip #153

"Wishing to be friends is quick work, but friendship is a slow ripening fruit."

In this tip, friends can also mean associates and networks. Networking is so valuable to career opportunities inside and outside of your organization due to information sharing. The internet is so powerful because it allows us to share an abundant catalog of information with one another in a short amount of time. Networking is a careful relationship where you need to provide value first instead of try to receive value. If you're trying to network with a person of greater influence, the key is to offer information, talents, or resources that the person can use. You want to be seen as a resourceful asset and not a user. You can't beg your way into opportunities. You can't automatically expect a hook up for one small act that you perform. Networking doesn't work that way. It's why more than 90% of people fail to gain any significant benefits from networking. They can't overcome their selfish tendencies.

Tip #154

"It is simplicity that makes the uneducated more effective than the educated when addressing popular audiences."

When there is a mixture of college and high school graduates in the organization, there is always concern with effective communication and perception to the audience as a whole. A college graduate can easily sound condescending and vain while using sarcasm and a "5 dollar word" vocabulary. Five dollar word vocabulary refers to using industry terms and professional terminology to appear brilliant and impressive. In actually, dialog delivered in a seventh grade level vocabulary may not undermine the intelligence of both groups if a few "5 dollar words" are sprinkled with laymen term explanations so no one is excluded from the conversation.

Tip #155

"To perceive is to suffer."

First impressions are dangerous especially in interviewing for new members to your organization. The look, the tone of voice, the body language, the body type, how clothes fit the person, among other things are observations that we evaluate inside the first 30-60 seconds of meeting someone to generate an impression or opinion of that person. As an interviewer, the intent is to find someone who can do the current job opening with the ability to grow into more prominent roles down the line and also find a personality that can work within your current environment. If you have to spend a lot of time with the person, it should be with someone that you could like on an interpersonal level. A pretty face with no substances gets old and stale quicker than you think. Although a homely person can't control their features, they can control clothes, personal grooming, and other personal appearance features.

Tip #156

"Anybody can become angry — that is easy, but to be angry with the right person and to the right degree and at the right time and for the right purpose, and in the right way — that is not within everybody's power and is not easy."

E-mail doesn't allow the reader insight into the mind of the writer. The reader is only allowed to read the message in whatever state of mind as they opened the message. This is where e-mail becomes a dangerous weapon of choice. Even if you could retract the message before it's opened, you wouldn't in the heat of the moment. E-mail has become a shield for a passive aggressive, brash, and introverted personality to voice strong messages without the face to face interaction. It is very easy to write tough if you can't see the person. You've received the advice about not responding to an e-mail in anger. It's better to call the person to fully interpret if the message was indeed written with a purpose to anger you. The person may be a poor writer that can't communicate their thoughts in a more professional way. If that is the case, give some coaching tips on how you interpreted the particular e-mail and how it could have been written to create a more well received response.

Tip #157

"The educated differ from the uneducated as much as the living differs from the dead."

The educated person has a diploma that shows that this person learned the fundamental techniques and practiced some theoretical applications in the specific degree chosen. In today's society, we qualify educated to refer to a college degree but in actuality, there are a lot of college educated folks that exhibit lower intelligence and common sense than a high school graduate or

GED equivalent. Education is important because the emphasis is placed on the ability to learn and think on your own if you have information available. The uneducated person prefers to be spoon fed information and told what they should or shouldn't do. The uneducated person doesn't want responsibility for what life brings to them. The truly (self) educated person takes on a more active role to understand themselves, how they contribute to society, and how their decisions impact organizations at large. The difference lies totally in the responsibility of decision making.

Tip #158

"Educating the mind without educating the heart is no education at all."

Success in high school depended on good memorization with a little practice on application. Good students were competitive against one another so they had a better chance to attend the college of their college. The average high school does not teach students to be community servants. You learn to be competitive and engage the mind but those practices when transferred to the working world actually can work against you. If you've never engaged in community service or played a role in a family where you weren't the center of attention, your emotional growth can be limited. You don't know how to give to someone. You may not understand that person use emotion constructively and destructively depending on their life experiences and roles of new people in their lives. As a leader, you need the engage the heart and minds of your team in unison to get above average results. One without the other results in headaches and wasting a lot of times figuring out how to get better results of them.

Tip #159

"Excellence is never an accident. It is always the result of high intention, sincere effort, and intelligent execution; it represents the wise choice of many alternatives - choice, not chance, determines your destiny."

Talent never separates good from great. The separation begins with the choice to be great. The next step is to continue putting in effort to become great on a steady basis. This effort is built on successes no matter how small. Congratulate yourself on the successes and use it as motivation to reach the next challenge. Choose to be great...just don't settle to be good. When you settle to be good, you become complacent and before you know it, you just got replaced with a person hungry to be great.

Tip #160

"To avoid criticism say nothing, do nothing, be nothing."

There are a lot of us that want to be loved and admired as leaders in our organization. We don't want any flaws pointed out. We want to be respected and admired. Sometimes, we say that we don't need to be loved...we want to be respected (and some may even say feared). I believe that leaders want to be liked. It is the social aspect of life that we want even if we don't want to admit it openly. Criticism is a natural occurring event in life regardless of your leadership role. The best leaders are criticized. U.S. presidents are critiqued and second guessed all through their administration. You truly can't judge how well a U.S. president performed his job until an administration or two down in the future to observe the long term impact of those directions without a critical political party eye.

Tip #161

"No great mind has ever existed without a touch of madness."

How many times have you heard that there is a fine line between sheer genius and pure insanity? The essence of this question and the tip above is related to thinking and linking objects and concepts that are not obvious on first thought. When you can remove the laws of science & old school opinions and then replace them with the dreams and boundary free thoughts of a small child, creativity explodes into innovative techniques and next generation technology. Current global decisions and world's natural resources will force society to become brilliant and innovative. Look at the evolution of cell phones over the past decade. Did you ever imagine that we would progress so far in such a short time? Think about where cell phone technology will be in the next 10 years.

Tip #162

"A friend to all is a friend to none."

This refers to the leader who acts like a politician; a lot of smiles, hugs, and empty promises. You may have good intentions to fulfill promises but if your fulfillment rate resembles a batting average, your folks will have confidence issues with your leadership and job execution. Team members look to the leader to help them get the necessary tools and resources to accomplish the team's objectives. If you're resource limited and seem unsuccessful to get proper tools for your team, it may not totally be the organization's fault. You may not be fully accessing your influence, creativity, and mastermind network to make it happen. Maybe your salesmanship to get what you need is lacking. Do you need to do more calculations to sell your point? Some executives are only sold by the numbers. Show and tell is a pretty powerful tool as well to convey a message of ignoring a current problem. Think about the managers that you need to secure those resources from; what is their motivation to act on their behalf? If the manager communicates by numbers and dollars, don't spend time on a show and tell because you like it. Don't just verbally convey your opinion with no proof and expect a resource constrained organization to jump with no evidence to back it up. Don't be a politician with empty promises; bring substance to your role and influence in the organization.

Tip #163

"Those who educate children well are more to be honored than they who produce them; for these only gave them life, those the art of living well."

Leaders are teachers, role models, and coaches. Leaders exhibit certain behaviors that resonate within a good team. Leaders offer the ability to create a generational impact. Remember Aristotle was the student of Plato and Plato was the student of Socrates. All three are considered among the top 20 philosophers of all time. I doubt there is any disagreement with that statement. Many feel that the Aristotle is a top 3 philosopher (if not number one). This is partially due to the impact of generational leadership. Aristotle even continued the legacy with teaching a very young Alexander the Great who grew to be a powerful king and part time philosopher.

Tip #164

"Patience is bitter, but its fruit is sweet."

At times, I feel that bureaucracy is a bad word. It seems to stall the speed of business. People involved in a bureaucracy will review the process but when in doubt, do nothing and wait for someone to react, come over, and explain it step by step to clear away the fog and dissipate the ignorance. At that point, they continue on to the next step in the approval. It takes patience and persistence to continue pestering folks within the organization's bureaucracy. In the process, the leader is presenting their ideas in different formats and learning how to answer questions in receptive ways to different audiences of various backgrounds. The bureaucracy is slow because those within are not well versed in all facets of the business and need better comprehension before acting on the request. The bureaucracy wants to be sure that the leaders have reviewed the benefits and consequences of the decision prior to submittal, all legalities have been considered, and can staunchly defend the value of the decision among the mountain of others in the suggestion pile. A bureaucracy functions as a safeguard against reckless personality who didn't do the right amount of homework before submitting their ideas up the organizational chain of command. When your ideas pass the bureaucracy maze of death, it is very fulfilling. You should continue to follow up and measure the positive benefits of that choice and use it for the next time as history and confidence builder to the organization. It could lessen the depth of interrogation before approving your plan.

Tip #165

"He who has overcome his fears will truly be free."

We place invisible leashes on our abilities and value within the organization structure. We stay within certain functions of the organization to focus on our strengths and not make our weaknesses vulnerable to the masses. We have fears of uncovering new abilities that may pay additional dividends because your knowledge base has widened instead of increasing in depth. Organizations will typically allow the young and unproven superstars to experience the breadth of organization functions in a quick world wind tour but the more established and impactful leaders will not receive the same opportunities. Fear has been expressed by the acronym as "False Evidence

Appearing Real". The organization and the leader both are in danger of losing out on valuable and expanded contributions because of fear and self imposed limitations.

Tip #166

"I count him braver who overcomes his desires than him who conquers his enemies, for the hardest victory is over self."

When a leader receives honest feedback from their peers and subordinates, it is a tough pill to swallow. The leader is vulnerable to really knowing what impact they have on their folks. We're all used to having managers evaluate our performance and provide feedback but some of our managers aren't around enough so we provide more of the picture to them to create an opinion. Your team is directly impacted by your leadership. Their opinion holds more value if they trust you and have no fear of repercussion. You learn what behaviors work well and what needs some work to get more contributions from the team. This was the intent of 360 degree performance feedback before employees would learn and manipulate the system to get better marks. An infrequent and anonymous request can provide excellent feedback but the leader must be emotionally strong to take it. The feedback is related to the actions and behaviors of the leaders and not the individual. We don't critique a person to destroy them. We critique to offer that person an opportunity for self improvement and organization gain.

Tip #167

"Those who know, do. Those that understand, teach."

Leadership is a two step process. The first step is to practice successful leadership in your function and organization. The second step is to teach others how to be a leader. You learned how to be a leader by participating as a follower. You observed the reactions of your teammates based on your leader's responses. You probably thought about how you would handle a similar situation whether it was good or bad. You learn as a follower and practice influence whenever you can. If not in your current organization, join a volunteer organization and hone your skills in that setting. Any practice is a good one. You will never master leadership. It is an on-going skill set that is built on a daily practice. If you're good, you will get the opportunity to teach your lessons to interested parties.

Tip #168

"The high-minded man must care more for the truth than for what people think."

Democracy is beautiful way to get consensus but the consensus choice is not always the best one. Leaders must review the benefits and consequences of decisions in question and go with the best choice. It may go against the grain of the consensus but provide a better option. As a leader, you will not be liked in these tough situations but you must make the best decisions and not the popular ones. Some popular decisions can damage the organization and put them on a course where it can recover.

Tip #169

"Even when laws have been written down, they ought not always to remain unaltered."

Policies are written for legal protection. They have unfortunately become laws that are self serving and bent to reduce risk as much as possible. It sometimes prevents an organization from being progressive and growth-oriented. Employees always feel awkward to approach the upper echelon about revisiting the value of certain policies and the true impact within the organization. Does it prevent the organization from moving forward thus falling behind the competition? Does it put us at risk with regulatory practices or inner company politics? Questions don't hurt unless it is asked in a threatening or unpolished way. Learn to carefully craft your questions and challenges to the organization to remove the defensive barriers and get a better understanding of policies. Practice asking your peers those questions first and then seeking advice to propose it in a different context for better consideration.

Tip #170

"All human actions have one or more of these seven causes: chance, nature, compulsion, habit, reason, passion, and desire."

One of the most important lessons for leaders is to understand their motivational drivers of their crew. Certain actions are bewildering to the leader. You wonder if your crew is sabotaging your efforts when there is broken communication between the two sides. If there is a decision that does not match up with your expectations, you need to have dialog with those individuals to understand the basis of the decision making. You don't blame or criticize the person. You're digging down to the drivers behind the decisions made. Was it made under traditional values, lack of available information, or malicious information? Check the seven causes when discussing with your crew and make mental notes when dealing with those individuals in the future.

Tip #171

"Whosoever is delighted in solitude, is either a wild beast or a god."

Good leaders need to be seen by their teams and keep the group engaged as much as possible. Presence is very important to the group. An absent manager makes a group slack off because the assumption is that the leader doesn't care. As much as a good leader need to walk around and make their presence felt in person, they also need to schedule some time in solitude. A really good leader use solitude as a time to schedule self mastery. You need a little quiet time to reflect on the daily activities, clear your mind of distractions, and evaluate the situations at hand. This is why you see a lot of leaders and managers stay late at work. Sometimes, it is the only opportunity to schedule some time alone to focus on tasks without daily distractions and a crew who needs to be in the leader's presence.

Tip #172

"Pleasure in the job puts perfection in the work."

When the leader creates a good environment complete with proper tools, resources, clear communication and a few perks along the way, your crew is happy and motivated. Well at least 80% of your crew will be very happy. You can't make everyone happy; that's utopia and real work life is not based in utopia. When an employee has a great environment, ideas are free flowing and the team is willing to provide extra effort without being asked; they just want to be acknowledged.

Tip #173

"Teaching is the highest form of understanding."

Be prepared to have your team members request to go to external training seminars and classes at your organization's expense. It's a ploy that many experienced subordinates will use to force the organization to invest in their career especially if promotion opportunities have been limiting to them. Younger subordinates also request these seminars to boost their resumes when headhunters start looking for talent. The trick to nullify 90% of those requests is to make an arrangement with the employee to fill out an evaluation of the seminar, prepare and deliver a training class to their peers based on the information learned. The average employee does not want to put that much effort for a few hours away from work. If they are unwilling to accommodate the request, they can't go. A truly enthusiastic employee will not have an issue with the request. They will take notes and enhance their own understanding of the subject by reflecting on the questions asked by their peers in a training environment.

Tip #174

"The aim of art is to represent not the outward appearance of things, but their inward significance."

The goal of a business is to provide a product or service for sale. Earn as much money as possible with as little investment as possible. A new facet of business lies in being a sustainable organization. We want our organizations and businesses to be profitable but reduce its negative impact to the environment as much as possible. Organizations should recycle, reuse, and be careful with its resources. Although the aim of business is to turn a profit, a successful business will turn a profit and be a benefit to society over the long term in sociological and ecological relationships.

Tip #175

"Learning is not child's play; we cannot learn without pain."

Although wisdom can be measured as much by learning from someone else's experiences as well as your own, some impressions are best felt personally. Experiences are a waste and provide no value if you can't learn from them. Leaders starting in a new area with an experienced group will sometimes run into a virtual wall. A leader will come up with an idea that was unsuccessfully attempted in the past but shows great promise. If you have a veteran team, they will be against it without any facts, documentation, and real memories of why it didn't work out. No one remembers the conditions; they remember the results. In this scenario, a leader should try it again and this time, record the conditions and the results. It should be documented and stored for historical reference whether it succeeds or fails so the next person can learn from it and make a wiser judgment.

Tip #176

"Dignity does not consist in possessing honors, but in the consciousness that we deserve them."

Leadership allows for mistakes; it is not built on perfection. It is built upon accountability and responsibility. When leaders make mistakes, we want them to own it and to say it. We want a game plan to make corrections and get back on track. A lot of managers feel to admit a mistake is to give the upper hand to the subordinates. As long as you don't have a habit of being overly critical or being too demanding, you should be OK with admitting fault. If you do share those character flaws, you need to a big boy or big girl and take the potential backlash with your head held high. You are not passing the leadership baton to a subordinate because you made an error in judgment. You are serving as a reflection of your expectations to your team.

Tip #177

"It is not enough to win a war; it is more important to organize the peace."

We consider some of our impressive teams and groups were the most competitive. They would compete against themselves, peers, other groups, and even around the world. Competition is a good thing as long as the competitive juices are aimed in the right direction. It is not good to compete with your team mates because it encourages selfishness and a risk of withholding information that could lead to a success story. It is not good to compete with groups inside of your own organization based on the same reasons. If the organization is set up to encourage teams to fight for the same resources and business, the environment turns into the "Survivors" television show. The only objective will be to win at all costs for your group but potentially cause the entire organization to remain limited in its business share because of a flawed philosophy. Instead of competition, the true intention of teams is to use the higher level of thinking which is based in creation. Create additional streams of income. Create additional uses to minimize inventory and other resources within the company. Create avenues to accomplish more in less time with updated technology, outsourcing, and streamlining process. Creation brings growth and innovation to a successful organization.

Tip #178

"Without friends, no one would want to live, even if he had all other goods."

All leaders need a mastermind network of mentors to share specific scenarios and get feedback on how to handle it appropriately. A leader without a coach is left to lead their group to best of their own devices which is limited. You should secure mentors that have life and leadership experiences which are more expanded than your own. It would be helpful to locate some of these mentors inside of your current organization as they would be familiar with some of the people, policies, and practices. If you don't have the privilege of local mentors, read biographies of famous leaders and self help books to create a virtual mastermind board of mentors. Think of it like a board of directors for your personal leadership brand (or the company of you, incorporated). Even the greatest athletes in the world need a coach to get them to reach peak performance.

Tip #179

"All paid jobs absorb and degrade the mind."

Jobs and careers differ from one another. You've heard that the acronym for job stands for "Just Over Broke". Jobs are believed to be a monotonous and ruthless grind of repetitive tasks performed over and over again on a daily basis for the length of the person's working career. There will be changes (good & bad) and technological upgrades that will frustrate the job community. Decision making with a job is a reaction based process. The motivation to do more is based on the leader's inspiration whether it is by carrot or stick. Careers offer variety in assignments. Careers actually offer an income ladder to begin climbing if you impress the right people. In a career, you may get the opportunity to make some of those decisions that impact the organization and leave an imprint. A career offers hope that you can have a better tomorrow while you hard today whether it is in this organization or another. A job is an exchange of routine labor for routine pay with no promises of security, wealth or legacy.

Tip #180

"For the things we have to learn before we can do them, we learn by doing them."

Theory is excellent but practical experience is even better. We learn by different methods. Some folks learn through the visual method; they have to see (illustrations, vendor drawings, etc.) and observe the work being done. Some folks learn better through the written word; they need to read manual. They compile and comprehend the information delivered in their mind to make sense of it. Some folks abide by the touch method; they have to put their hands on it to retain the information. They may be too hyper to read it and watch drawings but they can get in sync when the pressure is on for real life application. There may be a slight adrenaline rush to physically engage in a new process that is undefined to a new mind until it becomes a routine. Try to figure out what method works best for you and then apply it as much as possible. Try the other methods to see if your retention remains the same or decreases.

Tip #181

"To write well, express yourself like the common people, but think like a wise man."

You don't need to be long winded and verbose when communicating to your team and extended group. Messages should be concise and to the point. Define the problem or situation and list the potential resolution. Feel free to educate your team with as few words as possible. They shouldn't feel slighted or withheld from information but they shouldn't feel overwhelmed either.

Tip #182

"We make war that we may live in peace."

There is an old school thinking that if a process is not broke, then don't try to fix it. Leave well enough alone and focus on real problems that are headed our way. In an environment of continuous improvement, you can not afford to be content and complacent. Like a healthy and loving relationship, you can't be content with the same old thing; you have to spice it up a bit and try something new. Be willing to take your relationships and business to higher levels. Sometimes it seems like a war to mess with the predictable but it is brought on to create a greater peace.

Tip #183

"The whole is greater than the sum of its parts."

One of the biggest benefits of teamwork is that synergy generated under teamwork creates the mathematical formula of $1 + 1 = 3$ instead of the traditional value of 2. This can happen if the scientific value of 1 is extended to 1.4. When 1.4 is added to 1.4, the value is 2.8 which can be rounded up to 3. Synergies are collaborations where ideas are stacked upon one another to be mixed and matched to create a world class idea. The role of the leader is to be present and be a facilitator to these world class ideas.

Tip #184

"All men by nature desire knowledge."

The foundation of the universe is built on the quest for knowledge. Knowledge is built on a collection of facts, experiences, and experiments. The depth of a good decision lies in the quality and quantity of information available. Leaders will not have a catalog of information at their disposal at all times. They will have to randomly make a decision without a sufficient amount of information. The hope is that there is some general knowledge and wisdom that can minimize the risk of the decision. Afterwards, the better leaders start gathering information to develop the knowledge to know if the choice was solid or not.

Tip #185

"Misfortune shows those who are not really friends."

When a bad decision is made, you find out who has integrity, who exhibits fear and who has loyalty on your team. Hard times test you and your team's emotional and mental toughness. Some things can't be taught; it has to be experienced. Teams can't grow if there aren't hard times to endure and finding the strength within to live with their decision. A leader takes the bulk of the load but as a leader, you're more interested in the reactions of your team. Do they rally behind you and work on resolutions to dig out of the hole or do they stand back and wonder how you'll dig out of the hole by yourself? A scared team mate needs to be forced to grow up. They have to face their fears of repercussions and know that you'll stand by their side.

Tip #186

"Moral excellence comes about as a result of habit. We become just by doing just acts, temperate by doing temperate acts, brave by doing brave acts."

Be the best at whatever business you are involved in. Be excellent and be true to yourself. Be committed to the organization's cause. You don't need to devote 100 hours a week to your craft. You should work hard with whatever time that you choose to work above the minimum required amount of work hours. No one takes you seriously if you're talking about hard work and you don't work past 40 hours in a work week like clock work. We define those guys as clock watchers. The start and stop times are more important than the work involved. You can't be offended and threw a hissy fit if you receive a request that must be done today but it can in hour number 7 and it's a three hour request. As a leader, this is paying dues and honing your craft. You shut up and go to work. Managers gain confidence in you when you deliver no matter the circumstances.

Tip #187

"The Law is Reason free from Passion."

Rules are not made to be broken. It was made to regulate the trouble makers. Rules shouldn't be made based on emotion but behind closed doors, they are. You have to be cautious on setting up rules to catch the trouble makers which may represent roughly a small portion of your team. Those rules could be set up to catch your best players and force you to be fair on discipline accordingly or compromise your principles and let them off the hook which would diminish the team's opinion of you.

Tip #188

"Happiness is a state of activity."

Nothing is more rejuvenating than working on great projects that fall in the range of your expertise plus provide additional challenges to increase you and your team's skill sets. As a leader, you must keep your team members engaged especially your key personnel. To retain your best team members, you should have them prepare a list of dream and preferred assignments so that you can be on the prowl when the opportunity presents itself. Money is not always a motivator to keep a good talent. At times, your strongest players look for you to be fair, push all of the team members to step up their game, and offer them some nice assignments for growth. Happiness goes a long way to create a really good morale environment.

Tip #189

"Whatever lies within our power to do lies also within our power not to do."

Power is based on wisdom and understanding. It is packaged in the form of creative energy moving the organization either in a positive or negative direction. Not all managers are taught to handle power correctly. We assume that the title brings an instant pedigree to the person. We know that new leaders can learn how to handle power through mentoring and organization training. Create a practical leadership training program that presents skill sets necessary to perform the current job. If your organization doesn't provide this type of training, seek to outsource relative topics through external training organizations.

Tip #190

"Character may almost be called the most effective means of persuasion."

Upper management is geared to support winners. In the beginning of your career, you have no credibility and must prove yourself at any opportunity. You must provide facts and reasoning behind the decision. In the end, you must garner a good success rate that can be publicized and supply sustainable results. You need to create an accomplishments stat sheet that speaks for you across a diverse background in the management ranks. Your reputation will always be on the line but the line of defense should not be as stiff as it would be for a rookie leader.

Tip #191

"All persons ought to endeavor to follow what is right, and not what is established."

Long standing employees are steeped heavily in tradition. It makes sense that this crowd would be adverse to change and would go back into their play book to find solution to recurring problems. Unfortunately when tried and true answers are used to address recurring problems, the real issue looks at why we still have recurring problems. Obviously, we didn't identify the true root cause(s) and truly correct the issue(s). We can't ignore and stay running in the same old hamster wheel not going anywhere. We have to get creative and challenge traditional methods. We have to look beyond the old guard and put old problems to rest.

Tip #192

"Man is by nature a political animal."

Many corporate and public administration citizens treat their environment like a jungle. You have a lot of predators and political animals looking to survive and take advantage of personnel and different situations. A true leader understands the game of politics but is not obsessed enough to be a participant in the matter. If a leader does the right things, good things will happen to them. Leaders don't need to be soft and amiable to being run over. Leaders are firm and stand their ground to make a difference.

Tip #193

"It is during our darkest moments that we must focus to see the light."

We should be able to separate our home lives from our business lives. We should be able to accomplish this feat but we don't always adhere to the philosophy. When we have a distraction, it affects on our day to day decision making and the quality of our choices. It takes a high amount of focus and concentration to drive out distractions and maintain a high degree of effectiveness. This is one of the difference makers among the best in the business.

Tip #194

"Fear is pain arising from the anticipation of evil."

Business is as much about handling adversities and challenges as life but for some reason, we're surprised by circumstances in this arena. We expect our business situation to be boring and routine although we're capable of thriving when challenged. When the adrenaline rush hits, we fall back into the old fight or flight sequence. There is no two ways about it; you can measure the level of the competence and strength of the leader by the actions that are taken in those moments. You can feel the fear but do what is necessary to be done anyway.

Tip #195

"He is his own best friend and takes delight in privacy whereas the man of no virtue or ability is his own worst enemy and is afraid of solitude."

The way that a leader spends time (alone from the crowd) tells the level of effectiveness that they will have in their respective organizations. A leader cannot be so absorbed into the business that the business defines them. If the business falters, the leader isn't on suicide watch. Recreation is invaluable to the mind. Leaders need to distance themselves from certain scenarios and let the mind work without your awareness. Many problems were solved away from the daily fire fighting. Use solitude to reflect and center yourself before reengaging into the heart of the action.

Tip #196

"The energy of the mind is the essence of life."

When a leader is addressing a problem, blame is not the first step. Acting like a victim is not in the leader's vocabulary. The first step is to understand

and accept the reality of the situation. The mind has to be in sync with the situation. Good leaders know that they will survive and thrive in most situations. You need a positive mindset that you will succeed in any situation. It may not work in the way that you want but you will not give up before engaging in battle.

Tip #197

"Great men are always of a nature originally melancholy."

It is sad when you see upper level managers that are moving up with the chain with no real leadership skills. Their personality may be brash and obnoxious. Their knowledge base is out of touch with current reality or they were ignorant of the responsibilities of the position. In either case, it's frustrating. Do not succumb to the thinking that politics without talent will prove successful over the long term. Karma is a beast. What goes around, comes around but necessary in your timing. Be patient and focus on improving your skill set. Karma will bless you.

Tip #198

"The roots of education are bitter, but the fruit is sweet."

Knowledge is a beautiful thing but acquiring it is such a chore. When we are done with our school days, we are so happy to stop the learning process yet you should never stop learning. When you're done with the learning process, your career is about done. You'll condition yourself to a job. Change is imminent throughout life as well as business and learning is required to adapt to change. When you are resistant to learning, you are resistant to change. You cannot make an impact to business and society as a whole if you're not interested in learning new things and provide useful feedback to mold the present changes into future brilliance.

Tip #199

"All Earthquakes and Disasters are warnings; there's too much corruption in the world"

As a leader, you must learn to read your audiences. You can't provide the same message and treat everyone the same way. In general, everyone has different motives that drive them to move in the preferred direction. You can't communicate to everyone in the way that you want to be communicated to. You need to find out what drives your audience especially the key personnel. Some people are very detail oriented and want to be sure that you did your homework. Some people want to be sold and hear only the benefits & risks of the message. If you don't know the audience, sell the message in a concise package but have access to the details if requested. Be prepared so people believe that you are brilliant and on top of it.

Tip #200

"Time crumbles things; everything grows old under the power of Time and is forgotten through the lapse of Time."

Time gives way to the evolution of man and the brilliance within mankind. As technology advances so does the capabilities of man generating greater ideas. What is not lost to man is the legacy of the past generation of leaders. Famous and infamous leaders create a legacy that stands the test of time based on the expansion and limitations of future ideas. All decisions no matter how small are capable of a butterfly effect that can significantly impact the future of the business. The key is to understand the reasons behind the decisions of the past so it doesn't limit the decisions of the future. Nothing is more crippling to an organization than to be stuck in tradition without understanding the history behind the decision.

Tip #201

"Nature does nothing uselessly."

Every decision is made for a reason and not necessarily a good one. You will not agree with every decision made by the organization. You can't let your passion as a leader interfere with the affairs of the business. Many times, you hear that change often runs through the stubborn man. The stubborn man feels passionate and powerful like a force of nature. In some organizations, the stubborn man will eventually wear out their welcome and be dismissed in favor of a more amiable personality. The timetable for the stubborn man's demise is based on the level of influence, tenure within the organization, and strength of contribution to the bottom line.

Tip #202

"Learning is an ornament in prosperity, a refuge in adversity, and a provision in old age."

Each day offers an opportunity to learn something new. Leadership is based in continuous improvement. Continuous improvement is code for gaining success by avoiding inertia and complacency. Your brain must stay engaged and active in the present and future. When you have excitement and motivation, it boosts your energy levels and keeps you young & vibrant.

Tip #203

"The aim of the wise is not to secure pleasure, but to avoid pain."

The adage of working smarter and not harder is true. This doesn't mean that you don't work hard; you are expected to work hard…very hard. You are also required to use your intelligence and leverage your skills to outperform any person that could be in that same position. The game is to be a value added contributor and not a detractor. Businesses in similar industries are only different by the values added by the organization.

Tip #204

"Where your talents and the needs of the world cross; there lies your vocation."

Fulfill the needs of the organization and you'll always be in business. It's the first secret of starting up a successful business. The hard and easy part is identifying the needs of the organization and match where your true talents lie to match up perfectly. You don't need to lock yourself into one position for the rest of the career. This is a stepping stone for the organization to understand your commitment and discover the potential of your contributions in the long term. This is why learning over a career is critical to demonstrate that you will expand and grow right along with the organization.

Tip #205

"Man is by nature a social animal; an individual who is unsocial naturally and not accidentally is either beneath our notice or more than human. Society is something that precedes the individual."

The work environment is a social circle that functions like a dysfunctional family. We tend to spend more time at work complete with commute time than at home with our family and friends. You can select some people to be in your work circle but you can't choose everyone. You need some difficult personalities to challenge yourself and your thinking. Leaders need to understand the motivation of others and use that knowledge to communicate your message in the best possible way. A group of similar personalities will limit your approach and hinder your range of influence.

Tip #206

"Courage is the first of human qualities because it is the quality which guarantees the others."

It takes courage for a leader to hold folks accountable without laying blame. We want our crew to feel empowered and make decisions. We also want them to take responsibility and be accountable. It's a double edged sword where great decisions will yield high rewards but poor decisions incur consequences. Hopefully, consequences are appropriate to the impact of the decision and not over exaggerated. For your group, you exert control over the level of consequence. Your team needs to feel safe that you have control over your emotions and can assess the situations appropriately. This is best exemplified by your example as a leader to take responsibility and show compassion when teaching your team to perform the same acts.

Tip #207

"A tyrant must put on the appearance of uncommon devotion to religion. Subjects are less apprehensive of illegal treatment from a ruler whom they consider god-fearing and pious. On the other hand, they do less easily move against him, believing that he has the gods on his side."

Yes, jerks can be leaders in their organizations. We deal with them and they seem to succeed despite obvious flaws in their skill sets being noted. This is an example where their most important skill set overshadow the shortcomings of everything. That skill is the ability to pick an outstanding squad to work for them. When a team is so much stronger than its flawed leader, they will make the leader look good in hopes that the leader will be moved into another position. The bad part is the jerk will believe that they are the reason that their crew is that darn good. Indirectly the team is motivated by the jerk but it's due to spite the leader or should I really say jerk manager than be inspired by them. You will not know if you're the jerk manager unless someone tells you which is not going to happen. Why? No one tells the jerk except the pissed off employee or a sibling.

Tip #208

"He who cannot be a good follower cannot be a good leader."

Leadership does not follow in accord with the Burger King slogan of "Having it your way". You can't have it your way all the time. One of the most important facets of a leadership is to provide a good example. You can not expect your crew to wholeheartedly follow you when you verbally express your disagreement with upper management choices. It sends the message to your group that it's OK if they pull the same maneuver with you. I assume that the comments will be made behind your back in the same manner that they observe you performing the same act. We watch our leaders and take cues from the small lessons as well as the big ones in how to conduct ourselves. If you're not the top ranked leader in the organization, then you must serve as a good role model and show what an excellent follower looks like so they can follow the same mold. You don't want to be the "yes" person. You'll lose respect quickly at all levels. You want to be a respected and reliable team player that leaders want to have around.

Tip #209

"All who have meditated on the art of governing mankind have been convinced that the fate of empires depends on the education of youth."

Businesses love and hate youth as much as they love and hate experience. Creativity drives business to the next level and youthful exuberance is where it happens. Experience breeds tradition and can tie into a lack of creativity because business life, career aspirations, and politics beats the crap of an experienced business person. Unfortunately, a youthful employee has not witnessed a great deal of these circumstances and their future never looked brighter. A youthful employee will have to fight the hurdles of tradition and stifled thinking in their path to evolution of the society. We must identify and move towards progress otherwise we will regress.

Tip #210

"If things do not turn out as we wish, we should wish for them as they turn out."

Even the best laid plans have bumps in it, a function of business lies in problem solving. Some people call it firefighting. Firefighting can be stressful to the point of making you feel sick or provide that necessary adrenaline rush to get you going and feel alive. You know which type you are by reflecting back on your school days. When your teacher assigned you to complete a written report, did you finish the assignment a week or a few days ahead of time or did you complete it the night before? Whether it's pain or pleasure, our past can unlock the key to our motivations. The past doesn't have to define your present and future but if it goes unrecognized; it is likely that we will repeat the same behavior whether good or bad. Situations will repeat themselves to you over time in slightly different formats until you learn the lessons necessary to pass and move on.

Tip #211

"Through discipline comes freedom."

Self-discipline is within everyone's control. In the path to leadership, the first follower in your army is you. Choose a vice that is limiting you from reaching your full potential and address it. If you start a new habit and fail within a week, two weeks, or two months, don't beat you up; dust yourself off and try again. You must be willing to cheer and fight harder for yourself than you would expect anyone else to do for you. Discipline is the key. Respect yourself by your actions towards yourself. People will watch and admire you. And if they don't, you know that you are doing it which is good enough.

Tip #212

"The secret to humor is surprise."

No manager wants a surprise under nearly any circumstance. Surprise usually means problems...major ones. A surprise will typically be an inconvenient situation happening at an inconvenient time like a key personnel departure at the most crucial production time; a regulatory failure occurring right or during an inspection; someone ignoring a quality issue despite receiving the appropriate training. You can't control events but you can control your actions towards the events. You have a choice. You can either respond or react to events. When you react, you are more prone to go into a negative mindset looking to blame and lash out at the circumstances. When you respond, you are prone to go into a positive zone looking to deal with the current reality and confident that you can find a way out no matter what.

Tip #213

"To lead an orchestra, you must turn your back on the crowd"

Managers are sometimes so caught up in attending meetings with their superiors; they miss the group that needs their true focus which is your team. Your team needs your leadership and direction. They need to be aligned and move in harmony like a sweet playing band. It is a tricky slope because your manager is trying to communicate effectively with you but the time commitment sometimes overwhelms you to the point that you miss communicating to your group. It becomes a break in the communication tree which is bad. You need to spend time with your manager to understand the company's strategic plan and daily requirements. You also need to make time to communicate those same requirements and strategies to your team mates and ensure that they communicate the chain as well. When time is short, establish a 10-15 minute (on-the-spot) daily crew meeting where you can fill them in on the daily happenings. It doesn't have to be in a formal setting or meeting room. It just needs to happen where your team is together so they can feel in tune with you and the organization.

Tip #214

"With respect to the requirement of art, the probable impossible is always preferable to the improbable possible."

Leaders are considered miracle workers and magicians at times. We even surprise ourselves when we work through seemingly impossible tasks. At times, it is truly a matter of will to make the tasks at hand work to our advantage. It can be attributed to the quality of our team members or uncovering an advantage to mitigate the extent of the nerve wrecking issue. Some people call leaders lucky but luck can be defined as the intersection when preparation met opportunity.

Tip #215

"Man is a goal-seeking animal. His life only has meaning if he is reaching out and striving for his goals."

There would be no point in playing professional sports if no scores were kept, no records were broken, or no championships to be gained. We need these markers as fans and athletes to accomplish something. We need to celebrate and conquer challenges. We need to measure ourselves against greatness and see how we stack up. You cannot get stronger if you don't know your starting point. We risk becoming failures and unable to lead anyone anywhere because we're lost without a plan. As a leader, you must refuse to have your time wasted. Your activity must mean something. We need goals to focus our efforts in a positive direction otherwise we fall into chaos and accomplish nothing.

Tip #216

"Wit is educated insolence"

Every organization has a smart ass. That person believes that they are witty and charming maybe even likeable. This may not be the case in all organizations. That person could be classified as immature and disrespectful. For newer and younger leaders, you must be careful when exhibiting your wit. Be contrite and add in a comment here and there after a more experienced and respected person leads off. Don't be the first one to kick it off and find judgmental eyes veering in your direction. When you go out for drinks with colleagues, only drink enough to stay more sober than the rest of the crew. You want to be sociable but not the main story of the evening. Watch someone else lose their peer's respect rather than put yours at risk.

Tip #217

"It is not once nor twice but times without number that the same ideas make their appearance in the world."

Experienced employees cannot stand repeat ideas that failed in the past. They will not give the idea another chance. It failed in the past and they don't remember why. They don't remember what factors were involved, what talent level was involved, or how it was supported. The memory and emotion of the incident removes the fact that there is no recorded history to document the occurrences of the past trials. You can't learn from the past if no information is available in the present other emotion. A good idea is a good idea no matter when and how many times that it occurs. The important lesson for leaders on this subject revolves around understanding the background behind the decision. If we understand the root cause(s), we can make a wise decision and not repeat past mistakes.

Tip #218

"The least deviation from truth will be multiplied later."

When a leader withholds information from his team, it will have consequences depending on the content of the information. Any business related information should be communicated to the team. As a leader, you have control over how the message is delivered but it is your responsibility to deliver it. When information is not shared, there is an empty space waiting to be filled. In an empty space, a vacuum will appear replacing business dialog with rumors. The rumors will grew at alarming rate and become a tumor to the organization. Although leaders are supposed to have broad shoulders and shield the team from distractions, leaders can create a distraction if they create a distance between themselves and the team members. Remember the leader is the messenger. You control how the information is disseminated.

Tip #219

"There is an ideal of excellence for any particular craft or occupation; similarly there must be an excellent that we can achieve as human beings. That is, we can live our lives as a whole in such a way that they can be judged not just as excellent in this respect or in that occupation, but as excellent, period. Only when we develop our truly human capacities sufficiently to achieve this human excellent will we have lives blessed with happiness."

If you are reading this book, it makes sense that you are validating your desire to be an excellent leader inside your organization. You understand that you must first be excellent in your duties and skill sets before you can command a team. Aristotle followed a lineage of great students and teachers which shaped Western philosophy that founded in knowledge and driven by excellence. You knew 90% of this information before you read in any one of all the organizational leadership series. You needed to reaffirm yourself that you were on the right track. Well you are and I anticipate that bigger and brighter opportunities are in store for you in the future as long as you keep these principles close to you.

Ultimate Organizational Leadership:

6 Tips from Alexander the Great

Who is Alexander the Great?

(Born 356 B.C. and died 323 B.C.)

Alexander the Great is considered one of the greatest military generals in history. He was the son of a great military general and king from Macedonia named Philip II. Alexander's name derives from the term, "defending men". The fearless young leader was a student of Aristotle for three years as a teenager. He studied the arts and sciences and made himself very well rounded.

Alexander believed himself to be the son of Greek God and had no problems embracing his ego. He expanded his father's vision upon death and captured numerous   He also believed that he must serve as the ultimate role model for his troops. He suffered with his troops and lived in similar conditions during his conquests but celebrated and reaping the benefits with his team. Admittedly, he did reap more benefits since he was the leader. The undefeated general ruled Macedonia as king and was a pharaoh in Egypt.

Alexander believed that he was destined to be a leader of men and create the next dynasty. He built his organization with the intent to be not only good, not only great; he wanted to create the ultimate organization that could defy all odds and succeed.

Here are 6 tips from Alexander the Great to help towards Ultimate Organizational Leadership.

Tip #220

"There is nothing impossible to him who will try."

A positive mental attitude is the first ingredient to resolve any issues that you're facing. Yes you must understand your current reality but you also need to be psychic and see into a better future. A negative attitude only delays the inevitable which is success. The question is whether you will be leading your team to success or will someone else. You have to believe that you will succeed against all odds and engage your team to follow suit.

Tip # 221

"I am indebted to my father for living, but to my teacher for living well."

Whether we like or not, each boss cast an imprint on your behavior as an employee. Good managers instill good traits and experiences to your present and future career endeavors. Poor managers instill poor habits and bad behavior. Our first manager may have the largest impact over the course of our careers. You may have had a few or a multitude of bosses at this point but the chances are great that you remember your first boss whether good, bad, or indifferent. At the beginning of my career, I was ignorant in exhibiting good work habits. I had a good attitude and wanted to do a good job but was ignorant in the execution and seeking answers for growth. My first boss had a very honest and crucial conversation that I'll always remember and spurred my turnaround into a more valuable contributor within the organization.

Tip #222

"I am not afraid of an army of lions led by a sheep; I am afraid of an army of sheep led by a lion."

There has been a debate for the ages regarding leading a team laden with talent and questionable attitudes versus a team with a great attitude and work ethic who needs effort to overcome talent deficiency. Which group do you prefer to lead? It is not an easy answer. A talented team makes things easier. The sheer volume and quality of work of this group can be on a higher level. A talented team can convert a mediocre manager into a superstar leader. The problem is talented folks seem to carry baggage. Sometimes, it makes neurotic and overly passionate in their exploits. If the manager is not strong enough and can not tap positively in their subordinate's psyche, the talented team will become dysfunctional, scattered focus, and perform on a significantly lower level than expectations. Teams with great attitude and exuberant optimism will not fail and will not let down their teams if they can help it. A good leader can take this group and has a good shot at knocking down a lot of obstacles. They can be a good influence on incoming team members with a high level of talent.

Tip #223

"I had rather excel others in the knowledge of what is excellent, than in the extent of my powers and dominion."

Leaders are secure enough in their abilities that they can focus on developing their staff without feeling insecure and concerned about job security. Leaders realize that organizations get stronger through the depth and talent level at their base level rather than solely at the top positions. If the front line employees understand the purpose and drivers of the organization, they can take interest and at times, provide really good ideas to further move the organization in the preferred direction.

Tip #224

"How great are the dangers I face to win a good name."

One of the differences between leaders and managers is the willingness to take risks and excel in spite of them. Scared managers will not take risks because of insecurity and the fear of failure. Scared managers look to make excuses and pass blame. They want to be forced into action rather than be in front to lead in the journey. Leaders may or may not initiate the goal but they do grab the bull by the horns. Leaders take accountability and responsibility of their actions and their team. They are front in the line to receive the spoils and rewards as well. You know the cut between the leaders and managers by the amount of back talk from managers about the leader.

Tip #225

"Remember upon the conduct of each depends the fate of all."

The respect of the people lies in the character and integrity that the leader exhibits in the small daily events as well as the toughest of times. If the leader is condescending or breaks their word on a daily basis, it encourages the team to mimic the same behavior. Business is filled with hypocrites. Maybe it is intentionally done; maybe it is not. Although a lot of managers are not called on it, subordinates are watching the conduct of their leaders and taking note. Is this behavior necessary to move up the ladder? Will I be rewarded for selfishness or servant hood? As a leader, you set the tone for the behavior. They are watching you even when you're not paying attention. What kind of example do you really want to set for the next generation of leaders moving forward?

Conclusion

Whew, 225 quotes and interpretations on Organizational Leadership from the greatest philosophers and one of the greatest generals of all time. We know that at the heart of organizational leadership is to focus and drive to create and maintain a smoothly running process. Organizations are composed of a community filled with individuals utilizing more of their potential and contributions to drive their respective organizations to greater success.

There is a well-known and retold story of Socrates teaching a young man about the secret to success. Socrates had the young man meet him near the river at morning light. Socrates asked the young man to walk with him into the river. They walked until the water reached their necks. By surprise, Socrates took the young man's head and pushed him under the water. The young man struggled but Socrates was strong enough to hold him down. As the young man was in desperation mode thinking he was going to die, Socrates pulled his head out of the water. The young man gasped and took a deep breath. At that point, Socrates asked the young man, "What did you want the most when you were down there?" The young man replied, "Air". Socrates said, "That is the secret of success! When you want success as badly as you wanted the air, then you will get it!"

When you want to lead an organization and reach your potential as badly as you want to breathe, no one can stop you. You just need to invest your time, find the right tools, and go to work. I hope to learn how these 225 tips helped you on your journey to self improvement in future correspondence.

Thank you for investing your time and Good luck in your career.

Justin Tyme

www.ingramcontent.com/pod-product-compliance
Lightning Source LLC
Chambersburg PA
CBHW070258190526
45169CB00001B/460